FAREWELL RAJ

01902 - 324984

The Chimneys,
15 Penleigh Gardens,
Wombourne,
WV5 8EJ.

Dear Mr. Barratt,

Sorry you could not attend the launch which was very well attended — and far exceeded expectations.

The book is being reviewed in London in two London papers this month as a "classic" & I hope you enjoy reading it. —

Cost of book. £10 instead of £11-95 Please make cheque payable to H.A. Hearne.

Thank you.

H.A. Hearne

FAREWELL RAJ

TONY HEARNE

To Alan Barratt.
With Good Wishes.
Tony. Hearne
29. 3. 09.

TOMMIES GUIDES

Tommies Guides
Menin House
13 Hunloke Avenue
Eastbourne
East Sussex
BN22 8UL

www.tommiesguides.co.uk
First published in Great Britain by Tommies Guides, 2009
© 2009 Tony Hearne

ISBN 978-0-9555698-6-9

Cover design by Tommies Guides
Illustration shows detail from the Sikh parade at the Gateway to India,
28 February 1948. IWM HU 66178
Typeset by Graham Hales, Derby
Printed and bound in Great Britain by CPI Antony Rowe,
Chippenham and Eastbourne

Contents

Acknowledgements

THIS BOOK virtually wrote itself so vivid and life changing were the events it relays. The chapters tumbled out fully formed with sights recalled in bright colour and sounds with pristine clarity.

Moving from the handwritten jottings at the kitchen table to a completed book was never going to be easy.

My thanks go to my daughter Sharon who sifted through the original handwritten manuscript, arranged the typing and checked the spelling and the sequence of events. The first typed script required much re-reading and grammatical checks which took most of spring of 2008. Although this was laborious work the time we spent together as father and daughter has been time to treasure.

I am much indebted to Mr Peter Rhodes, senior columnist for the Express and Star a well respected and widely distributed newspaper in the West Midlands, for his favourable and encouraging comments and for printing 4 extracts of the book in February 2008.

I have received much encouragement along the way and have been heartened by those who have shown interest in this man's story. Without the efforts of my daughter and the encouragement of the publisher, family and good friends along the way the original dog-eared sheets would have remained in the cardboard box in the bottom of the wardrobe.

Tony Hearne
November 2008

List of Illustrations

Introduction to the Author

THE LAST of five children, Tony Hearne was born in June 1926 of the union of Gerald Frederick Hearne and Nellie Ethel White who were married in Agra RC Cathedral in 1911.

His early education was delivered by the nuns in the Jesus and Mary Convent in Lahore and later in The Sacred Heart Boarding Convent in Dalhousie until 1935, where his sister Olive Irene (the middle child) also attended for many years.

In 1936, Tony was sent to a boy's boarding school, St Georges College Mussoorie, under the supervision of the Irish Christian Brothers, to whom he has been indebted all his life for a good education. Two of his elder brothers were in the same school while he was there. Though not a brilliant scholar, he managed to attain the Senior Cambridge School Certificate in 9 subjects in December 1943.

During WWII, his three elder brothers served in the forces, two were commissioned and went on to be full time soldiers, one in the Canadian Army.

His mother, served as a nurse in the British Military Hospital Lahore Cantonment and his father was reemployed under the Defence of India Rules into the Controller of Military Accounts Office having retired from the Civil Service and his magisterial job at the age of 60.

In February 1944, Tony enlisted into the Army Ordnance Corps from whence he was discharged in August 1947 for a brief period during the events of this narrative. He re-enlisted in January 1948, again in the Royal Army Ordnance Corps, now the Logistics Corps.

Tony completed his service in August 1968 having risen through the ranks to Warrant Officer Class 1, and received, by Royal Warrant, the appointment of Conductor of Ordnance, the most senior non commissioned rank in the British Services.

During his serving years he enjoyed travelling to exotic places for long periods, among them India, Bermuda (3 years) Singapore and Malaya (3 years and Cyprus (3 years). He was also seconded to the Third Armoured Division for the Suez Crisis in 1956. Tours of duty were always accompanied by his late wife Doreen Mavis Andrews who never complained about the regular packing up of the home and moving to some far off place with daughter Sharon.

In subsequent years he served in equally exciting places, though in much harsher climates, including Iran via a secondment to the Iranian Army through the Crown Agents for the Colonies, now Ministry of Overseas Development and Kuwait with the Kuwait Oil Company, through Moody International of Haywards Heath.

Finally, after 5 years in Saudi Arabia with an American Corporation and AEG Telefunken, he hung up his desert boots in August 1984, and devoted himself to enjoying a well earned retirement and committing his memories to paper. This task which has taken some 20 years on and off having been fitted in between long holidays and tending his garden.

The loss of his dear wife, in 2004, was a severe blow, but this was tempered by his daughter Sharon and also by the friendship of a very kind lady companion, Irene Haycock.

Tony now lives in Wombourne in South Staffordshire and continues to enjoy a happy and active retirement.

November 2008

Chapter 1
Quit India

"JAI HIND – Jai Hind – Jai Hind", which started as a gentle chant some thirty years before the outbreak of World War II, culminated in a roar. The battle cry, in the early days, was the sole uniting factor of the many religious sects, Hindus, Muslims, Sikhs, all of which had but one objective in their sights, to get the British out of the subcontinent. The British had ruled India with a Victorian fatherly benevolence for some two hundred years, not without considerable affection and tolerance, but firmly and occasionally harshly, when the necessity arose, but never brutally.

Having the British around in the Civil Service, police, railways, post and telegraph, irrigation, medical services and above all the military, had long been accepted by the local population.

The British enjoyed the very obvious advantages of the most senior posts but also the more congenial aspects of colonial social life, with their special clubs reserved exclusively for the ex-patriots or covenanted hands as they were referred to.

These were the rewards for creating a reasonably stable society, introducing new technology and maintaining communal peace between the religious sects.

The chants and rumblings grew in volume, reflecting the discontent, and civil disobedience and passive resistance spread. The 'Salt March', led by no less a figure than Mahatma Ghandi, made a major contribution to the increasing unrest. The Government responded by bringing in more stringent measures to control the unruly mobs. Long curfew periods were instigated, the police and army were instructed to fire on the more violent and

11

destructive crowds, arrests were made and ring leaders jailed without trial. Much later, many of the participants in the final talks about independence were amongst those jailed, not least Mahatma Gandhi himself.

These general rumblings of discontent directed at the British administration were, from time to time, interrupted by inter-communal disturbances between Muslims and Sikhs or Sikhs and Hindus. On most occasions, these events assumed serious proportions with the burning of buildings, looting, innumerable killings and the desecration of places of worship. Under the Defence of India regulations, the local District Magistrates had considerable powers to call upon the state police chiefs and army commanders to take whatever action was necessary to separate the factions and restore order. It was during these periods the British were again temporarily looked upon as the fatherly figure that had successfully separated the fighting children and put a stop to the carnage and killing: until the next time. So the love/hate relationship continued uneasily, with long periods of calm, but the rumblings grew louder every year. These increasing tensions were almost disregarded by the British Parliament back home, who were more preoccupied with events of a different nature taking place in Europe where Hitler and Germany were the principal actors on the stage in 1938-39.

The declaration of war against Germany in September 1939 and the entry of Japan into the conflict in 1942 had placed the highest trump card into the hands of the All India Congress Party, who were the motive force behind the independence movement. The movement leaders were quick to grasp the reality and serious predicament of the British army in North Africa, and the unrelenting advance of the Japanese forces through Indo China, Malaya, Burma and impending entry into India through the back door of Assam.

The Congress Party were not slow to realise the vital importance of the Indian Army, which in the main, though commanded by British Officers was made up of fighting troops, entirely of Indian origin.

The Indian Army far out numbered the British regiments stationed in India, who in any event, could neither be withdrawn to help in North Africa nor were they strong enough to stem the advance of the Japanese in Burma and Assam on their own. Their main task was to maintain stability in India.

The loyalty of the vast majority of the Indian Army to their officers and to the King of England was indisputable. Ill equipped and insufficiently trained for warfare on a grand scale, as they were, they would have followed their officers to the last man, even if a deal had not been struck between Whitehall and the Congress Party.

The Colonial Office and Whitehall in their uncertainty of the loyalty of the Indian troops, and faced with an almost disastrous military situation on two flanks – North Africa and Burma – coupled with the fear that Congress may spread revolt among the troops in India, were forced into a situation of making a deal with the Congress Party. In return for the assistance of the Indian Army, in the now wide-spread theatres of war, India would be granted independence on the successful defeat of the enemy. However, the promise was vague, with no time limits or conditions imposed by either side, particularly in light of the fact that the final outcome of the conflict was uncertain. The commitment was sufficient to secure the services of the Indian Army in every theatre of war and pacify the majority of the Congress Party, although some would rather have done a deal with the Japanese by inviting them in, to get rid of the British.

The dissidents in the party, by this time, were having some success in persuading a significant number of the Indian troops to throw down their arms and desert to the Japanese.

The Indian Army's contribution to the 1939-1945 war effort was invaluable and their courage and bravery in battle is legendary, they served with distinction wherever they were sent.

The war years were comparatively stable, with the inevitable inter-communal clashes continuing in the large cities. Meanwhile, the dissidents in the Congress Party, impatient at the long drawn out war in Europe and the Far East, kept the pot boiling with passive resistance, civil disobedience and sabotage, constantly reminding the British of their rash or realistic promises.

It is arguable, that no other political or historical event in the 20th century except, perhaps World War 2, has been so comprehensibly documented, as the handing over of power in the first British colony to gain independence.

The serious student will find an Aladdin's cave of information in the archives of the old Colonial Office. Many books have been written on the subject and the biographies of the main participants, Lord Louis Mountbatten, Pundit Nehru, Mohammed Ali Jinah and Ghandi give different perspectives on the same subject. Each participant had different objectives.

Jinah was trying desperately hard to split the sub-continent and create the state of Pakistan; Nehru and Gandhi wanted to keep the status quo with power sharing for the minority sects; the British, who were watching the situation steadily get out of control, wanted to shuffle off, as painlessly and as quickly as possible, the responsibility of the transfer of power. No one suspected the situation would erupt into a state of chaos and anarchy.

The suggestion, made at The Simla Conference, of a five year period for a smooth administrative handover, was unacceptable to those, who by 1946-47 were hungry for power. The conference ended in complete failure.

The war had been over for eighteen months; the British Army was withdrawing from India as rapidly and as cautiously as possible, bearing in mind the chaotic conditions that existed in England and Europe. Industry and homes had to be rebuilt and work found for the half a million plus men who were being disbanded. The Indian Army, which came to assist the war effort, was also being reduced and the soldiers returned to the villages and fields from whence they came.

There was no rebuilding to be done in India which had suffered no material damage as a consequence of the war. Manufacturing had been greatly expanded during the war years and was stronger and more able to absorb some of the demobilised Indian soldiers, who had learned new skills during their period in the services.

As a result of the breakdown of the Simla Conference, Lord Louis was recalled to London and was virtually given total authority by the Labour government (Clement Atlee) to push through a settlement as quickly as possible.

Early in May 1947, Lord Louis returned and promptly announced that Independence would be granted in August of the same year. The political bargaining and demands of all concerned are well documented in official records and I could not possibly add any significant details. The subject has been covered in several books, television series and films including "Gandhi" and the less serious "Bowani Junction", all of which add to a vast overall picture, but none of which, could individually, give a complete account.

Chapter 2
Old India Hands

OLD INDIA hands, both military and civilian, more than sixty years on (the numbers are dwindling) still get together and swap tales about the old days. The once young conscript soldiers remember their service in India more vividly than any other period of their lives, and will, at the first opportunity, spin you a yarn and exercise the few remaining words of Urdu that they remember. The old soldiers (1925-35) will tell you of their tough life on the North West Frontier and skirmishes with the Pathans or Affrides in Baluchistan, whilst living in military bases as far apart as Peshawar and Quetta. There will be a few still around who defended the Beau Geste type forts at Landikotal and Kohat and marched through to the Khyber Pass. If you listen carefully and watch the expression on their faces you will detect a note of pride in their voices, a quivering in the throat and even possibly a tear, hastily wiped away with the back of the hand.

Life for the young British soldier in pre-war India and during the war was hard. Completely cut off from family and relations back home, they lived in stark prison-like barracks, surrounded by ten foot walls, in Birdwood Barracks, Lahore, or the slightly more congenial surroundings of Victoria Barracks, Rawalpindi, or in hundreds more like them spread right across the country. There was a great deal of discipline, a lot of spit and polish and little leisure time.

Every major town had a military garrison or cantonment area where the military spent most of their time training and maintaining their equipment. Living arrangements were mostly segregated from the local population except for the "Char Wallah", the "Dhobi" and the young "Chokra" boys, who earned a few annas a week cleaning boots and the interminable brass-ware which seemed to be dull again no sooner it had been cleaned and polished and never to the satisfaction of the Sergeant Major.

Part of the garrison was continuously on standby to rush in and break up the latest outbreak of communal trouble. The men of the garrison were always in danger of being hit by the thousands of missiles, including stones and bottles, hurled by both sides of the rioting mobs.

Sometimes, even that was preferable to the boredom of the barracks, as they nearly always had to penetrate deep into the city bazaar area, normally out of bounds. If they were off duty, they would most probably be lying on their beds in the sweltering heat of 108F or more, languid and mesmerised by the slow backward and forward motion of the huge canvas flap. The flaps were suspended from the high ceilings and were operated by the "Punkha Wallah" pulling a rope over a series of pulleys, and served as a primitive fan. The overall effect was nothing more than to keep the hot dusty air in motion and disturb the swarms of flies into settling elsewhere. Occasionally someone would hurl a boot or direct a volley of abuse at the punkha wallah who had fallen asleep on the verandah, with the rope between his toes and tied around his ankle, using his leg as the motive power for the fan.

The young soldiers, if they were lucky, might get an invitation from one of the local girls working on the garrison (Women's Army Corps India, WACIs for short), to go to the Railway Institute or Telegraph Club for the regular Saturday night dance, and five games of "Housie Housie", during the interval, when the band had a break and refreshments were available. Small groups of soldiers were invited by these clubs every week and it was a great reward to receive a pass from the Sergeant Major, usually accompanied by a twenty minute lecture on behaviour, drinking too much, and fraternising with the local girls too closely. Following a last minute inspection of turn out (uniform) and the threat of the cells for causing a rumpus at the club, there would be a dash to the barrack gates and a waving of passes under the nose of the duty sergeant. Waiting outside the gates would be a fleet of tongas, a two wheeled horse drawn conveyance, with tonga wallahs (drivers) pushing and shoving to get a fare, while the soldiers bargained to get the lowest price. Five rupees, four, three and eventually, three or four eager, beaming fresh faced young men would pile into the tonga for a fare of one rupee and eight annas, and a night out, probably the first for months. They would spend the evening having a bottle or two of beer, a game or two of Housie (bingo), three or four dances, conducted like two tailor's dummies, almost at arms length, under the watchful eye of mother, father, brothers and older sisters, to ensure no hanky panky.

If they were on their best behaviour they might end up with an invitation to a Sunday curry lunch and further nights out at the club. At worst, they would be escorted back to barracks by the military police (Red Caps) who were ever present, watching and waiting, for the slightest infringement of good military social conduct.

By contrast, army and senior civil service officers enjoyed a far higher quality of social life. Most had their families with them and their children benefited from the high standard of education available in the boarding schools and convents in the lower reaches of the Himalayan mountains, Srinagar in Kashmir, Dalhousie, Mussoorie, Naini Tal and Darjeeling to mention but a few. Some children, pre-war were returned to England at a very tender age for their education. They were cared for by relatives and spent many years separated from their parents.

The schools were situated in the summer hill stations for the troops. All were deliberately located at between 4000 and 5000 feet above sea level, away from the blistering plains where fathers and mothers sweated it out, unless they were fortunate enough to move to Simla, the seat of the central government during the summer.

During the cooler months, the officers and their wives back on the plains enjoyed the facilities of the gymkhana clubs and Officers' Mess, Sunday Tiffin, polo, tennis and tea dances. Some even got away on shakare (hunting) for tiger, buck, wild boar and ducks, or fishing in the many rivers in India for marsheer (Indian trout, a bit larger, but a great fighter).

Don't take too seriously the story of the old major at the local when he starts to tell you about the man eater he stalked for days and finally shot at point blank range when it pounced on him unexpectedly out of the tall elephant grass. He has, like many others, been reading the exploits of Colonel Jim Corbet who earned the reputation of the greatest tiger hunter in India. He later became an equally famous conservationist of the tiger and other wild animals, but only after every Maharaja, state ruler, governor and brigadier had had his photograph taken, rifle held across his chest, one foot on the animals head, and the tiger had almost been hunted into extinction.

My own childhood was idyllic, nine months of the year, March to November, was spent away from home at boarding school, first at the convent in Dalhousie and later, when I grew too big for my short pants, in St. George's College, Mussoorie. Both were beautiful hill stations away from the heat of the plains. I was a poor scholar but the devoted attention of the nuns and Christian brothers saved me from being a total dullard.

Every conceivable sport was available, football, hockey, cricket, volley ball, tennis, all the field and track athletics, boxing and swimming. But what I enjoyed most was the mid-term three weeks hiking and camping in the higher reaches of the Himalayas. The winter months at home were equally exciting, accompanying my father on tour to remote regions where he held court. I was out riding, shooting game, fishing or tracking the elusive snow leopard, spending a week or more sleeping out in the open with nothing more than the whispering pines and stars above me. My mother, a first class shot herself, faithfully kept my dad company on these trips, organising and directing the small retinue of guides and servants and making sure nothing was forgotten.

For the adults, the Christmas and New Year ball were exciting events, along with the twice yearly garden party and ball at Government House. These were the highlights of the social season. The feverish preparations for these events started months before and especially so for the ladies, who had to have new evening gowns for each function. It seemed impossible that this wonderful life style, unequalled in any other colony of the Empire, would within a few short years be shattered after a horrific sectarian blood bath, also unequalled in the history of the Empire.

This very comfortable state continued for a while after the outbreak of hostilities in 1939: it was not until Indo China and Malaya had fallen to the Japanese that the situation changed dramatically. Troops and materials were pouring in through all the major ports in India, Karachi, Bombay, Madras and Calcutta. Burma was overrun in spite of the brave but fruitless efforts of the 14th Army of Generals Slim and Wingate of the Chindits.". The Japanese were finally held in bitter, bloody, almost hand to hand battles in eastern Assam at Kohima and Imphal.

American troops and resources were pouring in faster than the ports could handle them. Ships were queuing up in the Hoogly River, down stream from the docks of Calcutta, fifty and sixty at a time. The docks at Kiddipore were working round the clock and the riverside jetties at Kali Ghat on the east bank of the Hoogly were fully occupied. No sooner was a jetty vacated than another ship was being pushed into position by the tugs.

Sheds and Godowns were chock a block with food, ammunition, weapons, vehicles, and were being removed as fast as possible by convoys of trucks, twenty four hours a day, to places of storage designated to store specific categories of material. No doubt a similar situation existed at the other ports. The fever of war was evident everywhere.

Finally the tide began to turn. The American war machine was in top gear and there were some materials to spare to supply the Chinese by air drops, over the "hump" in Northern Burma, from Barrackpore military airport some twenty miles from Calcutta. The old Dakota DC3 had a limited capacity so the heavy material and vehicles went along the Lido Road, a torturous quagmire for most of the way. The American, New Zealand and Australian troops were pushing the Japanese out of the Pacific.

Suddenly in August 1945 the war in the Far East was over. The European war had ended a few months earlier. Then started the huge task of dismantling the massive war machine and stock piles of material which were no longer required. This process continued for the next eighteen months. The Americans disappeared very rapidly, the ships stopped arriving in such large numbers, the systematic demobilisation of the British army was in progress, based on a demobilisation date related to age and date of enlistment. The Indian Army was also being reduced.

During this period the politicians had been haggling, demanding, threatening, without any agreement. Frequent violent communal disturbances were taking place in the major cities. Calcutta in early 1947 was experiencing the most violent and prolonged communal riots the city had ever known. The destruction, looting, burning and killing was unprecedented.

The depleted numbers of British troops in the city were once again pressed to the limit to try to separate the Hindu and Muslim communities. A couple of regiments stationed at Fort William and another from Barrackpore, plus soldiers normally employed on administrative duties were pushed into internal security duty patrolling deep into the bazaar area of the city.

The Indian Pioneer Corps was used to recover the bodies from every other alley where there had been hand to hand fighting between gangs, or some unfortunate individual had strayed into hostile territory and been set upon and beaten to death. The mutilated bodies sometimes in an advanced state of putrification were regularly recovered from the sewers. It was not unusual to see half a torso protruding from a manhole, which when removed invariably revealed four, five or six bodies thrown beneath. Grappling hooks or a bamboo pole, with a butcher's hook affixed, were the only way of recovering what was sometimes difficult to identify as a human body.

It was not uncommon to see a pack of dogs fighting over a human limb, or kites swooping down to pick up the entrails of a recently disembowelled victim. Three days in the sewers with the enormous rats doesn't leave much to be identified.

The British troops usually in groups of six or seven, with a corporal or sergeant in charge, stood by on guard while the pioneers got on with the gruesome task of loading the bodies unceremoniously on to the back of cargo trucks to be removed, at the end of the shift, to the communal burning ghat. There was no time to get involved in the niceties of identification. The sergeant merely kept a tally of men, women and children, and whether Hindu or Muslim, if he could categorise them by their dress. These patrols went on twenty four hours a day for ten weeks, with upwards of six hundred troops deployed continuously in groups, in the decaying, smouldering garbage and rubble strewn streets; the stench would often bring on a bout of vomiting.

I took my turn with these patrols, and being a Sergeant at the time, found myself in charge of a party as frequently as two and sometimes three times a week. We continued to carry out our normal administrative duties during the day and went out on patrol at night.

The details which are most vivid in my memory are the awful stench of the rotting rubbish; the dark nights (no street lamps); the slowly drifting smoke like a heavy sea mist penetrated only by the headlamps of the trucks; the ghostly appearance of the patrol moving about in the semi darkness with faces half hidden by handkerchief over nose and mouth in a vain attempt to keep out the smoke and stench; the pioneers fishing in the sewers and briefly examining the bodies by the headlamps so that I could add another stroke to the body count in the appropriate column; the young solider bending over and retching till his stomach muscles were knotted into a ball; the pariah dogs moving nervously about, waiting to snatch any dismembered limb and drag it away into the darkness; the enormous sewer rats, by the dozen, still clinging tenaciously to the remains of a corpse while it was being hauled onto the truck.

All the British troops were armed for their own defence and it was not unusual for bricks and petrol bombs to be thrown at our vehicles. The nightly tally rarely fell below four hundred bodies recovered and three or four burnt out vehicles. The bodies were despatched without delay to the burning ghat about twelve miles north east of the city on the banks of the Hoogly where the Pioneer Corps and engineers were kept fully occupied disposing of the bodies with diesel oil and paraffin. A huge pall of dense black smoke hung over the area and the stench of burning flesh could be detected long before reaching the site. The remains, after each "burn up", not always completely incinerated, were pushed with a bulldozer into the river where it was hoped the turtles, eels, and catfish, would complete the work. The great fear at this time was the possible outbreak of a cholera or typhoid epidemic, always a possibility at the best of times, which, if it had broken out would have raged with devastating results through the population in a congested city the size of Calcutta. The burnt out vehicles were recovered by REME (Royal Electrical and Mechanical Engineers) and closely parked in an open area the size of two football fields just off Chowringee in front of the Firpos Restaurant.

The casualties among the troops were mercifully small in relation to the numbers deployed. The greatest damage was probably psychological as many of them were among the last to be conscripted and had been too late to witness the horrors of the battlefield, but here, in what was supposed to be peace time, they were being exposed to the slaughter of civilians, night after night, for weeks on end.

I have witnessed many a healthy young soldier succumb to a bout of vomiting two or three hours before going on patrol, reduced to trembling and sobbing before boarding the truck that would take us deep into the city. Few words were spoken, each one dreading the next six hours which would force you to witness only a fraction of the terrible slaughter, brutality and degradation of a civil population, unleashed by a savage hatred, on those of a different religion. What those young soldiers experienced must live with them today, as it does with me.

May '47 found me in Calcutta where I had been for the previous two years with the Port Ordnance Detachment at Embarkation HQ Hastings situated in one of the nicer areas of the city.

Taking only a fifteen minute ride on the tram, skirting the western edge of the "maidan" into the town and getting off at the junction of Park Lane and Chowringee, you could explore the High Street or Crawford Market or do a picture show at one of the four or five excellent cinemas showing the latest Hollywood releases.

The Ordnance Club was next door to our billets and was the centre of social activities for the HQ staff and Ordnance Depot personnel from Fort William, only a couple of miles away. We worked hard and played hard and I remember many of the names and faces of those years ago and often wonder where the tide of life has taken them. Of one thing I am sure, they will remember those hectic nights at the club and at the "Green Hut", a fairly large recreational centre, built in the compound of Embarkation HQ. Big enough to have a bar and 30-40 couples dancing, it was built entirely with voluntary labour in our spare time from salvaged packing crates and wooden cases from Ballygung vehicle depot. The cases originally contained complete vehicles including the three-five ton GMCs in a "knocked down condition" which were reassembled in the depot. The paint, jungle green, millions of gallons now no longer required, was salvaged from the Ordnance Depot at Fort William where thousands of rusted, leaky drums were awaiting disposal.

Everyone seemed quite content until the outbreak of the major disturbances in early '47, which totally disrupted the social life and work schedules. Long hours on patrol in the city, after a couple of weeks, brought on weariness and a feeling of utter exhaustion. Sitting down to eat a meal was out of the question for all but the toughest and most insensitive. The stench of the city streets and the smouldering piles of garbage seemed to impregnate your clothes, hair and skin, and the sights of the previous night patrol, the decapitated and mutilated bodies would not go away from your mind's eye.

It was not surprising that the conversation soon got round to one topic, the next demob group number, and how soon they could get away. My own demob number was so far in the future that at the current rate it would have been June or July 1948 before I would have been eligible for release. However, about April or May '47 an Army Council Instruction (India) was issued which opened the door to early release, but not too many were prepared to enter. Oil had been discovered in Kuwait in 1939 but because of the outbreak of the war the wells had been capped for future further exploration and development. British Petroleum was now ready to go in to start work and required staff for a multitude of duties. In my eagerness to get out of the army and not fully understanding the conditions involved I applied for early release in June 1947.

Kuwait is a hostile environment, even today. Ironically I worked with the Kuwait Oil Company, after nationalisation, for three years, some twenty eight years later at their Ahamadi head office, where conditions were excellent. By then, many of the climatic disadvantages had been overcome with air conditioning in offices, modern bungalows, ingenious landscaping with brilliant bougainvillea, eucalyptus trees, cannas, date palms and first class facilities all round. I thoroughly enjoyed my time there and made friends with whom I still keep in contact. However in 1947 the picture was completely different: tin hut accommodation, no air conditioning, no roads, army style cooking and feeding arrangements, water rationing, flies, intense heat, dust storms, and bitterly cold winds in winter. I attended a preliminary interview, as a result of my application, at Kirkee Arsenal near Poona. There were only about six or seven of us present and following some simple oral and written examinations I found myself making the return journey to Calcutta with authority for immediate release. British Petroleum would contact me at my home address in Lahore with further instructions, railway warrants, travel documents and where to muster, (with others I presumed) and travel to Kuwait as a group under the protection of their umbrella. As we will see later on, these instructions never arrived and the direction of my life was changed.

The processing of my discharge was far more rapid than I had anticipated and with the declaration of independence only a couple of weeks away I was looking forward, in my ignorance, to the new adventure in Kuwait.

Chapter 3

Impact

THE FULL impact of the announcement of impending independence did not immediately take effect. The Indians were too busy fighting one another in the major cities up and down the country. In the villages and countryside the decisions announced in Delhi were so remote and complex that they were not fully understood by the rural population. The thousands of British ex-Indian Civil Service, Police and military officers who were long serving, some as many as twenty five or thirty years, who retired at the end of the war and had decided to settle in India, were in a state of turmoil.

There were large retired British communities living very comfortably in such idyllic places as Bangalore, Ooticamund, Dhera Dun and many other areas. They had over the years been lulled into a false sense of security and believed they would live out their retirement in comfort. No one really believed, in spite of all the talk, that Britain would ever give away the largest jewel in the crown.

It was the Anglo-Indian community, some half a million strong, who were now faced with the toughest decisions. They had formed the backbone of the Provincial Civil Service, Post and Telegraphs, Police, Railways and Irrigation Departments and were in every office where the government was involved, including the large UK based commercial organisations. More "British than the British" they had flocked to the three services voluntarily at the outbreak of hostilities in 1939, because it was the patriotic thing to do.

They had always looked upon England as the "Mother Country" without any expectations of ever going there. They had enjoyed the benefit of an excellent education in a great number of day and boarding schools and convents throughout India, which had been established by the civil administration. The schools, in the main, were run by Roman Catholic and Protestant religious organisations who were dedicated to the teaching profession including the Mill Hill priests, Jesuits, Irish Patrician Brothers, Sisters of Mary, Sisters of the Sacred Heart and many others. Long term colonial policy dictated that it was imperative to have a well educated, thoroughly loyal, indigenous population who would continue to fill the supervisory positions in all Government departments, for as long as India remained a part of the empire. At that time, it seemed forever.

The implementation of independence and the partitioning of the country into two autonomous states initiated a traumatic experience for large sections of the community. Very few had given any thought as to what they would do, where they would go, or how their lives would be effected, if at all, by the fast approaching independence day. Every social level of the population believed life would trundle along in the same old colonial way; cultivating the fields, harnessed for life to an avaricious and oppressive landowner, so heavily in debt that it would be impossible to clear in two lifetimes, or driving the express "Frontier Mail" to and fro on a section of railway which ran from Peshwar to Calcutta, or just sitting and enjoying a sun downer overlooking the neat rows of tea bushes of the plantation on the next hill. All this complacency and tranquillity was to be suddenly shattered by a disruptive force, the magnitude of which was far beyond the imagination of the various sections of the population. If any of the politicians either in India or back in the Colonial Office had any fears of what was to come, they certainly made no public mention of it, and much less of how to cope with it.

My own father who served in the Provincial Civil Service (Punjab) for some thirty five years and who I place among the more far sighted, had packed my mother off to England as early as April '47 to establish a home for the time when 'Jai Hind' became a reality. But he had also unfortunately, in 1945 made the earlier mistake of buying a tract of land in the Tehrai forest, 10 miles south of Dehra Dun, from where on a clear night you could see the twinkling lights of the two hill stations Chakrata and Mussoorie 30 miles away. He had spent almost his entire life savings on clearing the forest, building a bungalow and planting some thousands of grapefruit trees. Two army surplus generators provided domestic power and operated the pumps of the artesian wells for irrigation during the dry season. Fortunately the bungalow was not furnished and that expense was saved. He had installed a "chowkidhar cum mali" (watchman/gardener) and his family to keep his eye on the property, water the young grapefruit trees, generally to keep down the weeds, and stop the monsoon rain forest from reclaiming its domain.

Hassan Mansur Ali, the watchman, was a Muslim from the "Jat" (farmer) class, an ex Punjabi Regiment sepoy (soldier) whom my father had befriended because he had lost a foot fighting in the North African campaign. The "Old Man", as my brothers and I referred to our father (but dared only among ourselves) had been working for two years in the office of the Controller of Military Accounts (Pensions Division) in Lahore Cantonment, having retired from the PCS two years earlier when the war was over. Part of his responsibility was to chair the board with military doctors from the British Military Hospital to assess the percentage disability pension for disabled Indian soldiers.

Hassan was more than satisfied with his 120 rupees a month compensation, and his crudely made artificial foot, which enabled him to walk quite well with the aid of a walking stick. He was so pleased at my father's generosity (so he thought) that I think he would have given up the other foot for double the pension (a king's ransom to him) and this would have enabled him to take a second wife, which we think he did without any mention to my father, for fear of losing his accommodation at the bungalow.

The old man was well known and I believe well respected for his experience. He had often been called upon by senior officers of the I.C.S. and Indian Police for his advice on matters of local policy. In latter years before, he retired, he was District Magistrate in Rawalpindi 1937, Ferosepur 1941-1942 and Dharamsala 1943-1945 and cantonment magistrate in Lahore as far back as 1935. I cannot remember further back than that as I was just a "chicko" myself in 1935. If there are any around who remember him they will certainly be up in the 80s bracket. I particularly remember, as family friends, Mrs Alloway, widow of the late P Alloway (I.C.S.), Government Inspector of Explosives, (Northern Circle India) and Phil Johnston, Superintendent of Police (NW Railway Division). Alas, the "old man" is no longer with us but right to the end he too always had a story about India.....'Did I ever tell you about the time.....' He never touched a drop of the hard stuff before sun down, but like a lot of colonials, could down enough whisky in an evening to flatten an ox, a trait he must have acquired from his great grandfather, a ginger headed, ginger bearded Irishman, a military medico who was reputed to have stood on the battlements of the Residency at Lucknow during the Indian mutiny with a sabre in one hand and a bottle of gin in the other.

Of my mother's family we know rather less. Her father, an Aylesbury man, we know was a Colour Sergeant in the Oxfordshire and Buckinghamshire Regiment, who fought in the Boer War and moved to India with his regiment at the turn of the century. Her mother died in childbirth when her brother was born. Both children aged about 8 and 11 years in 1906, were placed in the Agra convent and made wards of the Reverend Mother Superior Eugenie and the Bishop of Agra. Her father was discharged from the army in India and worked on the construction of the Bengal Nagpur Railway in Assam as a foreman plate layer. He died in the jungles of Assam of black water fever about 1908 with no known grave.

George, my mother's brother, returned to England to live with an aunt and changed his name to Haskin. We know this, because many years later in 1920, my mother received a communication from the War Office saying her brother Private George Haskin had been killed at Flanders and had bequeathed his worldly possessions to his sister Nellie White: a watch, a ring, and six shillings in back pay. My mother was traced through the Bishop of Agra, who had remained her guardian right up to the time he officiated at her marriage in the cathedral in Agra in 1911. It was not too difficult to trace her, as by that time, she was married to my father who was a young up and coming civil servant, posted as assistant to the Inspector General of Hospitals Northern India.

My father 'met' my mother by passing little 'love notes' through a sympathetic friend who worked as a teacher in the convent attached to the cathedral. My mother had been brain washed into becoming a noviciate nun and sang in the choir which is where my father first saw her. These love notes continued for more than a year and the ceremony to confirm my mother as a nun was fast approaching. My father, after enquiries, approached with trepidation, the Bishop of Agra with the proposal that he would like to marry this noviciate nun.

A meeting was arranged with the Mother Superior and the Bishop present. Up to this time father and mother had not had an opportunity to speak to each other much less hold hands or steal a kiss. They sat on straight back chairs, back to the wall on opposite sides of the bishop's office, Mother trembling, eyes down, with nothing more expressive than a demure smile. Father, on the other hand, fumbled for words as to how he would support his future wife on his meagre civil service pay.

However, the proposal was put by the Mother Superior and my mother was given two weeks to give her consent or otherwise.

They never saw each other again until the second meeting a fortnight later in the same austere surroundings of the Bishop's office. My mother consented and they were allowed to hold hands – no hugs or kisses – the wedding was arranged for a month later.

The simple wedding dress was made by the other nuns from silk normally used for making church vestments. The bride was given away by the Police Commissioner, a friend of my father. There were few guests, mostly nuns and teachers, and the Mother Superior and the bishop who officiated at the ceremony. Life started in a very humble manner in a rented house in Agra with only a cook and a house boy to help the totally inexperienced bride.

From this marriage there were four brothers and a sister. My sister received her complete education at the Sacred Heart Convent ,Dalhousie and the four brothers all passed through the hands of the Irish Christian Brothers a St George's College in Mussoorie. They were dedicated educationalists and I owe them much. What you did not learn voluntarily they beat into you. I was not a good scholar and received a goodly share of the cane. I hated boarding school and was always in trouble for breaking bounds, scrumping cherries or apples from the monastery orchard, or having a prohibited catapult. I must have been a great source of worry to my parents as I eventually ran away from school, and had half the United Provinces and Punjab Police Force looking out for me on all the up trains to Lahore, some six hundred miles away.

I did my final year in St Joseph's College (Mill Hill Priests) at Baramullah, Kashmir, thirty two miles south of Srinagar; a more idyllic Shangri-La it would be difficult to find. It was only in later years I realised how much my parents must have deprived themselves to give all five of us a sound education in the best possible boarding schools, up in the mountains, away from the sweltering heat of the plains. My three brothers also served in the forces, two of them commissioned during the war and all three of us continued to be long serving soldiers earning pensions and melting away into civil life!

Thousands of families like ours were about to be plunged into a complete state of turmoil, with the mat of privilege, placed by the Colonial Office, about to be pulled, with little warning, from under our feet.

Independence was declared on 15 August 1947, and two new countries were born amid the beating of drums, bugle blowing, flag waving, ceremonial cannon fire and dancing in the streets. The 'Jai Hind' chant, which had grown over the years, was suddenly a roar so loud that no one for days even heard the calls for help from the minority communities in both new countries caught unprepared for the ugly change of mood.

The British were out, Pakistan was for Pakistanis and India was for the Indians. Millions of Muslims, and Hindus and Sikhs, official figures about twelve million, suddenly found themselves in hostile territory, where they had lived for generations in an uneasy peace with the majority. Now they were on the wrong side of a line drawn by the politicians to satisfy their ego, with a population who really did not fully understand what was happening. The retired British settlers were split two ways – "Let's get the hell out of here before we are all slaughtered in our beds", many arming themselves with pistols and shot guns, while the other half remained complacent, "Sit tight – we've seen all this before. It will blow over after a few weeks and life will go on just the same". The Hindus, Muslims, and Sikhs who were caught on the wrong side, were quite definite in what they had to do. They had to move to the other side as quickly as possible.

They abandoned everything except what they could carry, and moved by what ever means was available, train, bus or bullock cart, walking if necessary, as many hundreds of thousands set out to do. The British were no longer responsible for keeping the various factions apart and maintaining order. Indeed the slaughter was so wide spread, that even if the whole of the British element of the army had been pressed into service they would have been so thinly spread that they would not have been able to make any difference. They would also have become the target for both sides who now saw the British as the cause of their misery.

The Anglo Indians on the other hand, with stiff upper lips, learned from the British, tried their damnedest to keep telephones and railways running, until it was impossible because miles of telephone lines were pulled down and trains derailed by the score. Now they had time and reasons to worry about the loss of jobs, loss of pensions, half grown families and where to go to start a new life: would it be Australia, Canada or England. They were definitely no longer wanted by the Indians or Pakistanis, who looked upon them as the pampered servants of the British. Australia, Canada, and England (South Africa was out of the question) were not openly hostile but coolly reluctant to throw open the doors, as no one knew how big the flow would be, or what social problems it would create within their own populations.

The exodus could not start overnight as less than one in a thousand had a passport or even dreamed of needing one. Within weeks of independence being declared most had decided to sell up, beg, borrow or steal the money for a passage to whichever one of the three main choices would let them in. Many who were still serving members of the forces moved to England with their units, taking their immediate family with them. Over the weeks immediately following independence there was hectic activity: arranging documentation, medical examinations, finalising pension rights, or reclaiming contributions, getting the children out of the boarding schools which may, in some cases, have been on the other side of the new territorial borders.

All this had to be organised amid a complete breakdown of postal communications, telegraph and railways. Travel by road usually bus, was impractical, primitive and hazardous to say the least, not many owned cars and distances were great, petrol was still rationed and supplies dried up instantly.

Chapter 4
Farewell

O N MY return to Calcutta from Kirkee, near Poona, at the end of July 1947, armed with my letter of authority for immediate discharge from the army, I was overjoyed. This was to be short lived. I had already told my father, by letter, that I had applied for early release and that I was proceeding to Kirkee for induction. I had to return to Calcutta for discharge, and the onward journey to Kuwait, but I planned to come back home while awaiting instructions from my new intended employer. My father's reply to my letter was waiting for me on the letter board in the Sergeant's Mess. He strongly advised me not to go to Kuwait, with a long description of the harsh climate and tough conditions.

Kuwait was a protectorate of the British crown and he had been there on three or four occasions before 1939, to hold court and dispense what passed for British justice, travelling up the Persian Gulf by motorised dhow from Karachi. The journey alone was a feat of endurance: sleeping on deck, the scorching heat, the wild unpredictable storms of the gulf and the most primitive of feeding and toilet arrangements.

To add to his disappointment, the situation was even more complicated by the fact that my mother had returned from England unexpectedly, it was the last thing he wanted. My mother, alarmed by press reports in England, and in her blind loyalty to the old man believed, like a lot of others, that if all non Indians were going to be slaughtered in their beds, she wanted to be right there beside him.

Leaving the house buying arrangements in England incomplete, she boarded the first ship on which she could get a berth out of Tilbury in early

July 1947. It was an old freighter with cabin accommodation for six passengers only, and still bearing some of the scars of the war time convoy duties from England to Malta, and beyond.

During her four months absence, my mother found that the old man had sold up lock, stock and barrel except for the bungalow in Dehra Dun, for which he could not find a buyer: had finalised the transfer of his pension payments to the Pakistan High Commission in London and was living very frugally in anticipation of his departure. As it turned out, eventually it all took much longer than he expected, and the additional responsibility of having my mother out there under the circumstances that prevailed, all added to his worries.

It was now too late for me to reverse the procedure for my discharge, and in spite of the old man's advice, I was not sure I really wanted to, but I felt a little guilty at the thought that I was getting out of India leaving them to face the full fury of the months to come, or so I thought.

On the 12th August I was called to the orderly room and told that all the formalities regarding my release had been finalised and it only remained for me to hand in my kit and collect my railway travel warrant, discharge papers, final pay, my war gratuity and allowances in lieu of a demob suit.

The following day I handed in all my army issue clothing and uniform retaining only those items of khaki drill uniform which I had had made privately, the normal issue being so ill fitting. I would be on demobilisation leave for a further fourteen days anyway, and was entitled to wear uniform up to the end of that period.

I felt a peculiar twinge of becoming isolated when I reported to the armoury to hand in my Smith and Wesson revolver and twelve rounds of .38 ammunition which I had been issued with in January for personal protection and which had never been more than an arm's length away at anytime for seven months. It was always either slung from my army webbing belt, in its holster, during working hours, carried openly when on internal security patrol deep in the heart of the bazaar area or under my pillow fully loaded. I never had necessity to fire it in self defence as I was always on patrol with a squad of infantrymen and there was safety in numbers. However, I was not totally defenceless, but more of that later.

The next two days were spent in saying farewell to the many friends I had made in Calcutta including Barney McCarthy of the British India Steam Navigation Company, an old school colleague of mine. His widow still lives in Western Australia. Others included Willie Jewel and Mac McMullens, (late of Smith Instruments, Bishop Cleve, Gloucestershire), Dick Meakins, whose father was Commandant of the Ordnance Depot in Fort William and a host of others too numerous to mention.

There was a special farewell dinner with "Pop" Royan, (Marine Superintendent, Bengal Nagpur Railway at Kidarpore Docks,) and his wife Zoë, who provided very generously all the home comforts and hospitality I could ever have wanted. Their four lovely daughters Jean, Noreen, Corinne and Heather all married and had families of their own, now dispersed around England somewhere. All were unanimous in saying how lucky I was to be getting away so soon and wished me well in my new job in Kuwait.

Of course, I must mention one more good friend and drinking partner 'Jock' McPherson, a jute mill manager where I had spent many hours on security patrol, and with whom I did a regular monthly swap of one bottle of scotch whisky, still in short supply, for forty eight cans of Blue Ribbon beer.

I eventually sold him one of two Luger pistols I had acquired complete with two magazines of ammunition for his self-protection. His mill and adjoining house were in a notoriously troublesome spot in the suburbs of Calcutta. He had been in India some twenty years and had no desire to return to his native Dundee where he had done his training as a young engineer.

He had a young Chinese wife who waited on him hand and foot, cooking all his food herself, in spite of him employing a company cook, and spent hours behind his chair massaging his shoulders or sitting on the floor working alternately on one foot and then the other. She always made sure his drink was replenished the moment he put down his empty glass. I never heard her speak, but she understood every word he spoke in spite of his broad Scottish accent. His one desire was to retire to Ooti and raise pheasants as a hobby.

Independence was declared on 15 August 1947 and outwardly there was little to make it any different from the day before.

Those who had been on patrol on the night of 14-15 August encountered the same conditions that they had experienced for many weeks previously: the nightly killings, fires, stones and bottles and the gruesome job of the recovery of corpses amidst the interminable stench of rotting garbage. As every other night, the slowly rolling thick acrid smoke, hung like a sea mist on the hot humid air of the August night, shallowly penetrated by the headlights of the recovery trucks with their gory load. The rats scurried, as always, fat and bloated, from over eating on the abundance of human flesh and uncollected garbage. The intermittent attacks on the patrols persisted in the dark unlit alleyways with the inevitable casualties sustaining cut heads and faces or battered ribs from deliberately dislodged masonry falling from the upper floors of tenement housing. But there was never a target to fire at in the dark.

The corporal filled in his body tally by the headlights of the truck: three males – Muslim, two women – unknown, two male – Hindu, one male – unidentified, two children – unidentifiable and so it went on as they patrolled the city night after night. I was glad to be getting away.

On the 16th August I was once again called to the orderly room and informed that all my documents, pay and allowances were ready for collection, and that I had a reservation on a troop train leaving Howrah Station at 15:30 hours the following day. I was informed that after I had handed in my bedding and produced all my clearance chits from the Ordnance Club secretary, the Mess Secretary and the Quartermaster Stores, I could pick up my papers and depart by military truck at 14:00 hours on the 17th.

The 16th evening in the club was a hectic demob party for me, attended by those of my chums who were not out on patrol. After I paid all my outstanding dues over the bar, membership fees up to date, returned my membership card to the Club Secretary (Capt: Gee I.A.O.C.), I received the clearance chit with all the appropriate stamps and signatures.

The party went on, it seemed, forever. The gramophone was wound and rewound churning out the dance tunes all evening. The girls we knew who came in that evening as casual callers, to change library books or look at the magazines in the reading room, were invited to join the party. The members grew until there were about forty of us drinking and dancing and eventually singing.

Among the young ladies who came was Jennifer Burbage, daughter of Major Burbage DAQMG at Embarkation HQ. I had arranged to meet her at the club that night; she agreed to come if she could get away. Her mother didn't quite approve of me for some unknown reason, or so I believed. However, Jennifer put in an appearance but accompanied by her mother and elder sister Joan. The party was just beginning to swing and my chums were ribbing me that I could never get Jenny to join the party with the old battle-axe around. We acknowledged each other's presence with a demure wave and smile as she trundled into the library behind her mum and sister, clutching two or three books under her arm. I was really crestfallen as Jenny was at that time the love of my life, and I had wanted to say farewell on this my last night in Calcutta, with the hope that we might meet again in England, if and when I should ever get there.

A few minutes later, as I was watching the library door in the hope of getting another glimpse at her emerging, I was presented with a neatly folded piece of paper on a tray by one of the club waiters. The waiter, immaculate in his long white coat, white trousers, and turban, with a broad cummerbund belt in ordnance colours and brilliantly polished IAOC cap badge in his turban, urged me to take the note. I took it hesitantly, and the waiter (we always called them "boy" though all of them were grown men) was nodding his head in the direction of the library. I read the note, a one-line request ,"Tony please come to the Library", signed by Joan.

My heart was pounding; my knees went to jelly, with butterflies in my stomach. I didn't think I had the courage to face this older sister, and although she was probably no more than twenty-five or six, I was as much in awe of Joan as I was of her mother, as I was only about twenty-one. I got up from the table and started in the direction of the library, not really knowing what it was all about or what I was going to say. I did not know Joan other than that she was Jenny's sister, I had never spoken to her before, but we had nodded heads and briefly passed the time of day whenever we had been in the club. I had always managed to keep a respectable and safe distance between us.

I entered the library and there was Joan almost standing to attention, she was a Captain in the WACI. I said, "Good evening," nodding my head respectfully with a nervous constriction in my throat, that I thought would choke me, I don't think I actually heard the few words I spoke. She responded immediately, "Jenny and I would like to join the party if you ask mother's permission". I glanced at the counter where her mother and Jenny were signing out their new books and back at Joan. I couldn't speak; the ordeal of asking permission would have been beyond me, with the constriction in my throat getting tighter and a cold sweat breaking out. I must have been on the verge of making a dash out of the library back to the party, when I heard a gentle voice saying "Make sure you bring them home safely right to the front door, enjoy yourselves, and don't be too late." It was Jenny's mother speaking; I could hardly believe my ears. She turned to leave us, taking the books from Jenny. "I'll see them home myself, thank you very much", I said, almost bowing from the waist as though she was the Queen of Sheba, who had just bestowed a great favour upon me.

She made for the main exit and I took a few paces meaning to accompany her to where her husband was waiting when she said "Get along with you now and enjoy yourselves". I picked up Joan and Jenny, one on each arm, and we joined the party. That was not so bad after all I thought to myself, though I had hardly spoken. My chums were quite astounded that I had come over to the party not with one daughter but two. The two newcomers added to the dancing partners and the evening was really warming up. Joan had a couple of drinks and two or three dances to the squeaky gramophone, which could hardly be heard unless you were right next to it.

With a final wagging of her index finger at me, which said more than if she had spoken the words, she slipped away with her good looking captain fiancé from military intelligence. I had suddenly been given a great sense of responsibility towards Jenny who was only about eighteen, so I immediately curtailed my drinking and did more dancing, cheek to cheek, on the patio where the lights had been dimmed and the "boys" were going backwards and forwards with trays loaded with fresh drinks and removing the empty glasses. The party went with a huge bang; the yardstick of success being how many bodies were left asleep on the patio, slumped in the huge wicker chairs.

Jenny and I slipped away early and I walked her home the four hundred yards or so to where she lived: it was the first time we had to ourselves all evening. We were dutifully challenged by a security patrol on duty in the Hastings residential area and we were allowed to proceed. I felt the quarter mile was not long enough to say all that I wanted to. There was hardly time to exchange promises to write, and to take her home address, Coombe Down in Bath, before we found ourselves at her front door, with packing cases and crates stacked on the verandah, all neatly stencilled with their destination in England. The Major was also getting ready to depart from India, having done some twenty five years and nearing retirement age, he was retreating to his beloved West Country.

Our parting was tearful on both sides and after a few minutes on the verandah, her mother appeared at the front door to comfort her young daughter. She bent over and gave me a peck on the cheek and said I would be welcome at their home in England. So I said one final good bye and with a squeeze of hands turned and left, too full of emotion and wondering why I had been so scared of her mother.

I had to pass the club again to go to my quarters in the mess, but I didn't dare go in again, as I didn't want to start my travel day with a thick head. Those that still had the ability were singing loudly with slurry voices. As I covered the last few yards to my room I could hear the fading strains of "My bonny lies over the ocean, my …..".

I was soon in bed, having undressed, switched off the light, turned up the overhead fan full blast, pulled down my mosquito net, and feeling for the security of my illegally obtained pistol under my pillow. With a mixed feeling of happiness and sadness, I wondered what the future held for me, as I fell asleep for my last night in Calcutta.

Lord Louis Mountbatten planning the final details for the smooth handover of power in 1947.   *AP/PA Photos*

The author – far right on second step – at his boarding convent in Dalhousie 1933.   *Author's own collection.*

The author Tony, with his sister Olive, after church on Sunday at the convent in Dalhousie.

Author's own collection.

The young Tony with his sister's bike in the garden.   *Author's own collection.*

Tony aged 14 ready for church.   *Author's own collection.*

Tony growing up to be the young "sahib".
Rawalpindi 1942.   *Author's own collection.*

The author's sister - Olive Irene Hearne.

Author's own collection.

Pop Royan- Marine Superintendent at Kiddapore Docks Calcutta in 1946 and two of his four daughters – Corinne and Heather.

Author's own collection.

Colonial times - sister Olive with mother knitting and friends.   *Author's own collection.*

Author's parents in the cool of a summer evening - Lahore Cantonment Magistrate 1934-1935.

Author's own collection.

An entire settlement murdered raped and looted- atrocities on both sides of the border- the vultures prepare to attend the corpses. "The street was short and narrow. Lying like the garbage across the street and in its open gutters were bodies of the dead," writes Bourke-White's biographer Vicki Goldberg of this scene.

Margaret Bourke-White/gettyimages

Men move corpses from a truck in the aftermath of rioting between Muslims and Hindus. Estimates of the dead run into the thousands, while injuries run into the tens of thousands. *Margaret Bourke-White/gettyimages*

Chapter 5
Getting Away

T HE NEXT morning the house boy, that I had shared with Willie and Mac for two years, appeared at the usual time of 6.30 a.m. with three steaming hot mugs of tea, but he was quite alarmed that neither of them were in bed, he knew they had not been on patrol during the night.

He could read 'Daily Orders' on the unit notice board, as well as anyone, and knew exactly who was on duty, on what date and at what time and was constantly reminding us not to be late. I immediately sent him off to the club where he gained entrance through a little gate let into the tall hedge, and sure enough he found the pair of them, and a few others, still slumped in the wicker chairs or sprawled out on the settee on the club patio.

With some urgency he went around waking them up with a lecture about being late for work and being put on a 252 (AF252 charge report). The other house boys also knew the routine well and soon there was a small group of bedraggled uniformed bodies being herded through the little gate by a smaller group of house boys with the dexterity of a pack of well trained Welsh sheep dogs. I was in no hurry to get up as I was not going to work, so I let Mac and Willie go into the bathroom first to shower and shave, and get down to the mess for breakfast, while I enjoyed my second mug of tea in bed. Both of them had dreadful hangovers so there wasn't a lot of conversation. I soon followed and got down just in time to catch everyone hurriedly swallowing the last cup of tea before they dashed off to work. There were more brief handshakes and farewell wishes as I would not see most of them again.

It was a long morning, as I didn't have much to do. The houseboy folded up the blankets and sheets with the pillow on top and disappeared off to the quartermaster stores to hand them in and get my clearance chit. I waited in the mess for the treasurer to appear to check the bar stocks and collect the night's takings; there wasn't much, as most members had been in the club next door. I paid up all my outstanding dues, got my clearance chit and was about to leave, when in came the truck bringing back the previous night's duty patrol from the city. They were late in, as they had to call in at the British Military Hospital, opposite the racecourse, to drop off two casualties from the night patrol. The ambulance had been burnt out by a petrol bomb. Most of them would go straight to bed after a shower, not having the stomach to face a breakfast after the sights of the night before.

I ambled off to the orderly room armed with all the appropriate chits to collect my documents. "Don't go away, the CO will see you in five minutes," called Jack Normington, the senior warrant officer, a Yorkshire man who had married Colonel Meakin's daughter a few months earlier. "Okay Jack, I'll wait," I replied. I was duly ushered into see Major Conybere, if I remember correctly, under whom I had served the last two years. I gave the expected salutations in the smartest military manner and was directed to a chair. The usual thanks for services were rendered, "Sorry to see you go, hope you haven't jumped from the frying pan into the fire," he said, alluding to my going to Kuwait. Of course he knew all about it, as he had signed the documents. Another handshake and I left his office to make the final check that the duty truck was available to take me to the station.

"2 p.m. outside the mess without fail," confirmed the Mechanical Transport Pool sergeant. Out came the Indian drivers and fitters from the garage. "Mr Tony sahib is leaving to go home," said Kani Lal the head driver. There were more handshakes and "Salaams" (farewell greetings), all round. Most of them had at one time or another put a screwdriver or spanner to my Matchless 350cc, which I used to get me to and from work at the docks. None of them were properly trained, but all had a natural aptitude for things mechanical. With a lump in my throat and feeling very alone I wandered back to my room clutching a large brown envelope with all my documents to finish my last minute packing.

The room was stark and bare, Mac and Willie had laid claim to all my 'pin up' pictures taken from Esquire, and other magazines,. Betty Grable, Jane Russell, Anne Sheridan and the other original 'OOMPH' girls, each one displaying their particular charms as their contribution to the war effort, no longer occupied wall space.

I lay on the bare mattress for an hour with my head propped up on my small pack as a pillow, just looking blankly at the high ceiling through the whizzing blades of the overhead fan. I was turning over in my mind, all the places I had been and people I had met since joining up three years and 129 days ago as my discharge book declared.

I enlisted straight out of school in January 1944 where I had been struggling to master the principles of the dynamo in the physics lab, something about congruent triangles in geometry, plus "To be or not to be ... ..." and getting my ear tweaked for not knowing the soliloquy by heart. As I lay there thinking how quickly time had flown, how I had enjoyed most of it and how I would miss the comradeship of the services, I was suddenly brought back to earth by the reappearance of the houseboy. He looked like a new pin in a clean shirt and trousers, both of which I had given him, amongst other things, because I had no place to pack them. His hair was plastered down (with Willie's Brylcream no doubt), he was grinning from ear to ear displaying his excellent set of teeth which seemed whiter than I had noticed before. A large brown paper bag was put on the bed, "Haversack rations," he said. "I got cook to make special for Mr Tony sahib." I must admit the bag was larger than the mess cook usually gave out, but at the time I thought I could do without having to carry another package, as I had enough baggage to contend with.

He insisted on giving my shoes and cap badge one more polish, although he had done them only a few hours before. "Twenty minutes to two sahib, I put the baggage on the verandah." He struggled first with the heavy tin trunk, dragging it across the verandah to the top of the short flight of stairs, then the leather suitcase, well battered and scuffed on the corners from long service with my old man, then the half size tea chest which contained my gramophone and some records, well protected with cotton waste and wood shavings, and finally he went to pick up my small pack, bedding roll and the newly added package of haversack rations.

"Leave the small pack," I said, not wanting to leave it out of my sight as it contained all my documents and my war souvenir pistol. The latter was too bulky to wear in the shoulder holster under my bush jacket; it would have been too obvious to the sharp-eyed military police at the station. The houseboy returned with my shoes and cap badge which he gave a final polish on the seat of his trousers and replaced very exactly into my peaked cap. By the time I had paid him his wages up to date and given him ten rupees baksheesh, for all the odd jobs he had done, which he accepted with profuse thanks and more broad smiles displaying those excellent teeth, the truck had arrived.

As I took one last look around the room to make sure I wasn't leaving anything behind, I thought sadly about the innumerable late night sessions of pontoon and brag that had gone on there over the last two years. I strode out on to the verandah and was surprised to find the house boy and Kani Lal heaving the tin trunk into the back of the snub nosed Chevy 15cwt truck. It was a wartime design product of GMC Detroit with more pointed corners and sharp edges than a roll of razor wire, but sturdy and reliable nevertheless. Kani Lal usually drove the Commanding Officer or Captain Baker, his adjutant, but I didn't question the special treatment. I counted the packages and was climbing into the cab, dragging my over stuffed small pack behind me. "I come to station and help you with luggage to the train sahib." I knew the truck would have to return immediately. "How will you get back?" "On the tram sahib." "Ok then, get in the back." I was glad he was going to be there as I was dreading trying to find a platform porter with a barrow to move the load with every possibility of having a piece of baggage stolen in the process.

The truck moved off out of the mess compound, the Chowkidhar on the gate grinned and gave a very smart salute and a salaam. Hell, everyone seems to know I'm going, I thought.

The truck turned left on to the main road, instead of right, as I had expected. "Why are you going this way?" I asked Kani Lal, "Much safer this way sahib, Kali Ghat Road is dangerous, the small boys throw stones and bottles at military vehicles." That was a good enough reason for me. We had only gone two hundred yards when there was a knocking on the rear of the cab; I slid the rear window over. "Missy Jenny sahib, Missy Jenny left hand side," he said with urgency in his voice. I turned in my seat to wave good-bye to Jenny standing on the roadside. I had not noticed her as I was not expecting to see her, but Kani Lal slowed the truck to a stop right next to her on the footpath.

I climbed down and in the three or four steps I could see the tears streaming down her cheeks. Within seconds my throat was constricted and I could feel the tears welling up in my eyes. We both simultaneously held out both hands to one another. I took her hands, I bent over and kissed her on the cheek, neither of us could speak, my tears began to flow and with a final squeeze of her hands I turned and clambered back into the cab before I made a complete fool of myself. With my head out of the window it was the last I was to see of Jenny for many months, standing there on the pavement tears streaming and waving a tiny white handkerchief as the truck moved off again. Kani Lal just looked straight ahead, not saying a word, giving me a few minutes to blow my nose in the huge khaki issue handkerchief and to recover my composure.

The meeting, I am sure, had been contrived by the house boy with the collusion of the servants of the Burbage family. They had previously carried notes for both Jenny and me when we wanted to meet without her parents knowing. Of course, my house boy must have been the instigator as he knew in detail all the timings of my movements and Kani Lal had been drawn into the harmless conspiracy; he must have been a romantic at heart.

The truck turned left at Racecourse Corner on to the red road, named because of its surface colour – I never did know the correct name – which ran parallel to the tram track for nearly a mile, skirting the edge of the huge grassy maidan. Only eighteen months previously, the red road had been fenced in and used as a runway by the RAF as a Hurricane fighter station, right in the heart of Calcutta, for defence against any possible Japanese air attack. I took a last glimpse through the trees at the Victoria Memorial with the black marble angel atop the huge dome – the only virgin in Calcutta they used to say, because no one could get up there – it was a typical example of the extravagant colonial architecture at the turn of the century. Chowringee, on the right hand side, the museum, the Lighthouse Cinema, and Firpos Restaurant stood out amongst the line of shops. A huge car park of burnt out vehicles served as a reminder of weeks of disturbance. We journeyed down past the Cenotaph, at the other end of the runway, and Eden Gardens on the left, famous for its magnificent pitch and as a venue for test matches. The ornamental Burmese pagoda, brought all the way from Rangoon and faithfully reconstructed at the edge of an ornamental lake of covered in water lilies and alive with huge golden carp, represented the focal point of the garden. Half a mile further on, following a couple of left turns we reached Dalhousie Square, with its elaborate architecture in the form of the GPO and the huge government offices. The plaque on the wall of the Post Office marked, reputedly, the site of the infamous 'Black Hole of Calcutta', later expunged from the history books in the interest of good international relations.

One more left and right turn and into the last quarter mile of Kali Ghat Road, we crossed the massive structure of the single span Howrah Bridge which dominated the sky line. The bridge, with its dual carriageway separated by a double track of tram lines and was suspended from a spider's web of steel girders with overhead catwalks, bustled with thousands of pedestrians, horse drawn vehicles, buses, cyclists and rickshaws crossing in both directions.

Below in the filthy brown liquid of the Hoogly River, hundreds of devout Hindus stood waist deep, sloshing themselves, at the temple bathing ghat. Occasionally they completely immersed themselves and prayed in the hope of being cleansed of their sins and gaining entry to Nirvana, or whatever other heavenly abode they had set their hearts on. They were quite likely to get there sooner than expected through diphtheria or cholera, but the contradiction in terms of cleanliness, spiritual and bodily, never entered their minds: these were the sacred waters from the Ganges.

With the bridge behind us and bearing left through a warren of shanty streets with fragile corrugated iron and cardboard huts, huddled together and as insecure as a house of cards, we arrived at another architectural monolith not dissimilar to Waterloo Station in London, but ten times as dirty and a hundred times more crowded, Howrah Station.

The truck pulled up at the entrance, I clambered out to help lower the tail board and move the luggage. The driver remained seated, the boy and I struggled with the heavy trunk on the walkway and the rest was piled on top. One more jump into the back of the truck and the brown paper bag of haversack rations was retrieved. "Oh hell," I thought, I was hoping he would forget that and leave them on the truck in the hurry. An unkind thought I know, for which not too long after I was truly sorry.

We slammed the tailgate shut, put in the retaining pegs and with two bangs on the body work to indicate all clear, the driver moved off, waving as he went. "Stay here sahib," said the boy, and before I could reply, he had disappeared, after only a few paces, into the seething mass. I was surrounded by humanity, milling about. All seemed to be carrying pathetic little bundles on their shoulders or struggling with a suitcase, the women often dragging a couple of kids behind or precariously balancing a toddler on one hip.

It is to be expected to see people at a station carrying luggage, but this pushing heaving mass? Where the hell were they all going or coming from? I was to find the answer later.

While I was still contemplating this anthill of activity, I caught sight of the boy struggling to get through with a sack barrow. Together we loaded the luggage; I slung my small pack over my shoulder and carried the brown bag with the bloody haversack rations. It was not far to the main entrance of the station hall, a matter of twenty yards, but it took us fifteen minutes to negotiate a way through the crowds. I began to think about departure time.

Once inside the Booking Hall, it was not so crowded and I made straight for the RTOs Office (Railway Transportation Officer). I got to the counter fumbling for my railway warrant which I exchanged for a ticket, and produced my leave pass to the MP behind the counter. It was now 15:05 hours. The sergeant ran down a short list of names on his board, ticked off my name, and gave me the ticket. "Your berth is reserved, second class, platform one, it's a special trooper, no need to hurry there's been a slight delay in departure time."

I found the boy outside the office, dutifully sitting on the luggage, awaiting further instructions. "Platform 1," I said, and off he went pushing the barrow, swearing and barking at those who impeded his passage. We got to the platform and started to walk up the length of the train, beginning at the rear end, which was hard up against the buffers. The first three coaches were goods wagons with the doors open and sepoys loading stores and material. The next was the guard's van, then a double length coach which served as a cookhouse, two more goods wagons into which sacks of flour, rice and other dry rations were being loaded, then two first class compartments (4 berths each) and then two second class compartments (6 berths each). Looking at the reservation cards in a holder by the carriage door I saw HEARNE, IAOC NO: 4 and just two other names in 1 and 2, which didn't immediately register. I helped the boy get the luggage inside.

Bunk No 4 was on the other side of the coach, away from the platform and on the left side of the train in the direction of travel. Bunk No 6 was directly above. The leather case and the half tea chest easily went under my bunk, the tin trunk though was too high, so I turned it on its side and placed it in the walkway between bunks 3 and 4, with one end hard up against the wall. This still left about eighteen inches of walkway between the trunk and my bunk. I put down my bedding roll, small pack and rations on the bunk as a mark of territorial claim and went out on to the platform. I gave another five rupees to the boy for helping me; I hadn't seen a porter anywhere and would have had to pay that anyway if I had found one, more smiles and

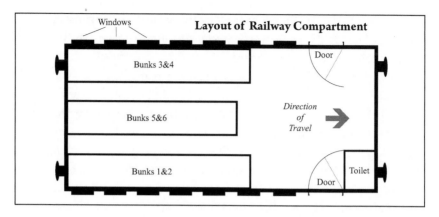

more teeth. The time was now 15:30 hours and loading was still going on in the goods wagons behind me. The RTO was dead right there was going to be a slight delay. Last salaams and handshakes with the boy and he went off at a run, and I wondered why.

Another unkind thought entered my mind: the little sod has pinched something and is getting away before I discover it. I automatically felt my back pocket for my wallet and went into the compartment to check my small pack; everything was there so I dismissed it from my mind.

I opened the bedding roll, which consisted of a quilt, blanket and pillow and spread it on the bunk in the form of a sleeping bag and set out to survey the compartment on my side. I tested all the sliding shutters; three to each window and door, glass, fine wire mesh and louvered. I left all the wire mesh in the up position to keep out the one million flies that wanted to invade; there was no one else in the compartment so I did the same on the other side. A twist of the fan switch, nothing happened, a flick the light switch, no lights: maybe we were not coupled up for power yet.

16:00 hours. "Damned hot in here, get a bit of air outside," I thought. With the small pack slung over my shoulder and with nothing to do but wait, I got out and started to walk up the platform. The next coach was empty, but with names on the reservation cards, and then I was surprised to find a locomotive, in the middle of the train, ten carriages up from the end. The driver and fireman, oily rags in hand, were busy doing their final checks. I walked past the hissing engine to the next coach which was third class and, as far as I could see, the next five or six coaches were the same. A second locomotive at the head of the train helped to share the heavy load of twenty to twenty two wagons and carriages.

Standing back from the coaches about twenty feet were sepoys with their havildahs (sergeants) and naiks (corporals) waiting to board the train with their kit bags and other equipment.

All very smart, a closer look revealed they were members of the Frontier Force Rifles, an all Muslim regiment recruited in the Peshawar area with many Pathans and Afghans amongst them. Interestingly, several of them wore the 8th Army ribbon, denoting veterans of the North Africa Campaign: excellent soldiers, loyal to the core. The whole regiment was returning to its home location, probably to be employed on security duties in familiar territory, or possibly to be disbanded, I didn't know. I was quite sure they would be glad to be going home after a long separation from their families.

Then I noticed a group of British Officers standing even further back, a couple of subalterns, two or three majors and one with red tabs on his collar, and a red band around his peaked cap, the Colonel. They seemed to be having a very serious discussion with a similar group of Indian Army officers and a couple of very well dressed Indians in light weight suits with ties but wearing traditional headdress. On the road stood a Humber staff car with the new national flag of India hanging limply from the right front wing. Affixed to the radiator grill was a red plaque with two five pointed gold stars. "Top brass," I thought, giving the regiment a send off. I didn't want to get any nearer, so was about to turn about and return to my compartment to sweat it out, when I noticed that the Colonel seemed a bit agitated, striking the palm of his left hand with his short cane and shaking his head from left to right as though saying, "No, no, no, a thousand times no." One of the civilians was waving a piece of paper in front of the Colonel. It looked more like an argument than a discussion as the others in the group were all sombre faced and standing back two or three paces from the Colonel, who from time to time turned to a British major, said something, got a reply, and seemed to repeat it to the civilian.

I turned and left to walk back to my bunk, passing the engine driver and fireman who were drinking tea from well-chipped white enamel mugs. "Cup of tea mate?" I looked up at the engine cab, it was the driver holding an equally battered white enamel tea pot as, if to say, its just been mashed. "Wouldn't say no," I said, as I started to ferret in my small pack for my mug. "Here you are man," he said, handing me a steaming hot mug as well used as his own: it was welcome. "Off on leave then man?" "Well yes and no," was my non committal reply. "Where you going man?" "Lahore," I said,

"Long way to go man, never been up north, no further than Delhi I been man. You've got over twelve hundred miles to go man."

Ask any old steam engine driver: it was a dirty job. Behind all that sweat and the grime on his face and arms and the heavy leathery tan, from long hours on the foot plate, he was, unmistakeably, one of the legendary Anglo-Indian drivers of the EIR (East India Railway), with an accent which often lead people to believe they were all Welshmen. We chatted on for a while, when I ventured, "What's the hold up?" "It's that fat little bastard over there man." He indicated with his arm still holding his mug. He had pointed towards the group of officers that I had been watching earlier. The only fat one there was one of the Indians in the lightweight suit, with a pundit 'chip bag' type of hat on his head. "Can't move man, till he gives me the all clear, some bloody Brigadier or General or something." I returned the mug with thanks. "Come up again man, anytime. We are bound to be shoved into a siding along the way." "Okay," I said.

I ambled back to my bunk and stretched out. The fans were buzzing and the lights on now. Thank goodness we've got power. I turned the lights off and lay down: my watch said 17:00 hours, one and a half hours late and no sign of movement.

I must have dozed off; the sultry heat and the soothing buzz of the fan were both responsible. I was suddenly woken from my short deep sleep by voices and movement in the compartment. Two VCOs (Viceroy Commissioned Officers) were hauling their luggage in and stacking it in the most convenient places. One of them was saying in Urdu "I don't like it, I don't like it, he should never have agreed to his demands." As I moved to get up off the bunk they both gave me a greeting. I manoeuvred my way to the door of the carriage between the cases, bedding rolls and other pieces of luggage and out onto the platform. I was just in time to see the troops lined up in three ranks just beyond the engine. One of the NCOs gave a command and I saw the troops ground arms – lay down their rifles on the platform muzzles pointing forward – another loud command and the front rank moved off in single file carrying their kit bags and started to enter the third class carriages.

They were soon followed by the centre and rear rank forming orderly queues waiting their turn to enter, all leaving their arms, rifles, Stirling and sten guns in neat rows on the floor of the platform. I looked towards the rear of the train and I saw large dark green and brown cases being removed from the last three goods wagons. I instantly recognised these, being an Ordnance Corps man, as cases of LMGs (Light Machine Guns – Brens) and 2 and 3 inch mortars. "What the hell is going on?" I thought. They were loading them only a couple of hours ago, now they are taking them off again. I re-entered the compartment where the two VCOs were still muttering away in their own language and laying out their bedding on their bunks. "What's going on out there subedhar (lieutenant) sahib?" I said in English. "Sorry sahib not much English speak." So I repeated the enquiry in Urdu. He was quite surprised that I could speak his language, but replied straight away. "Our CO has agreed that the whole regiment will travel without any arms." "But you still have your pistols." I said. "Yes, only British Officers and VCOs may keep their weapons, but I would be much happier if I had a Bren gun in my holster and two thousand rounds of ammunition instead of all this luggage."

At that very instant, there was a shrill blast on the whistle of the engine, I stood at the open door of the carriage and saw the stragglers starting to crowd the doors of the third class carriages lest they got left behind. Turning to look the other way, I saw the doors of the goods wagons were being hastily closed and bolted. Two or three minutes later, I heard a second blast on the whistle. I glanced at my watch 18:35 – three hours late – then, two or three sharp lurches of the train made me stumble and reach out for something to hold on to. Another short blast on the whistle, another two or three jerky movements and the locomotives took up the load.

The platform started to slip away as the train got up to walking speed. I could hear the furious hiss of steam from the engine (only one coach length away) and the grinding sound of steel against steel, as the driving wheels were spinning in an endeavour to grip the rail. The speed increased to a fast walk as the train gained momentum. Looking to the rear, the guard was standing on the running board holding the handrail with one hand leaning out as far as possible waving his green flag with all the authority he could muster.

I was now passing the rifles and other weapons laid out in rows on the platform and the highly polished leather bandoliers with the pouches containing ammunition, which were being collected by twenty or thirty Sikhs in military uniform. The train was now moving at slow running speed. "Sahib, sahib," I heard, I looked in the direction of the voice; it was the houseboy running frantically trying to get level with me. He flung off his shoes hardly hesitating in his run – he could run faster barefooted than with cumbersome shoes – he gained a few paces. "Don't go sahib, don't go, get off the train," he shouted breathlessly and then he began to fall behind but kept motioning me with his arms as if to jump off.

By this time the train was moving too fast anyway and within seconds as I saw him slowing his run to a halt. The end of the platform slipped away fast and I was looking down on a network of steel rails with points criss-crossing one another, it seemed, with the wheels whacking out the familiar dull clack clack, clack clack, clack clack, as they moved across the points to another rail. I stepped back from the doorway and heaved the heavy door closed and pushed the handle down to bolt it. The doors on all carriages on the Indian railway open inwards and could not be opened from outside unless unbolted.

I was puzzled by the actions of the houseboy and couldn't fathom out what could be so urgent. All manner of thoughts passed through my mind, but I could not come up with a satisfactory answer. I was still turning these events over in my mind, watching the sun setting low in the skyline, while half stretched, half seated on my bunk. The two subedhars were undoing their bedding rolls and mumbling away to one another, too fast for me to understand except the odd word here and there. They then, having removed their headdresses and footwear, spread out a prayer mat on the floor and standing side-by-side facing the sunset, and roughly facing Mecca they proceeded to say their evening prayers. I drew myself into the corner of the bunk and sitting motionless, so as not to distract them and as a mark of respect. I continued to watch the crimson globe slipping, below the horizon, with the innumerable coconut palm trees silhouetted against the sky and the still water of the lush green paddy fields reflecting the last rays of the sun. Within ten minutes of the sun disappearing it was pitch black – as is usual in the tropics. The subedhars were still praying, as I watched the myriad of fire flies over the fields and the occasional white hot pieces of coal which had fallen from the firebox of the engine bouncing away leaving a shower of brilliant red sparks in their wake.

Prayers over, the men stood up, rolled up the mats and switched on the lights, which were much brighter now, and the fans too were turning much faster, as we were now getting full power from the generators with the train moving. Up to this point I hadn't thought of food, although I hadn't eaten since morning: but when my travelling companions produced a tiffin carrier of pungent smelling Punjabi curry and naan bread I became aware of a vacant spot somewhere in my stomach. "Will you eat with us sahib, it is only a simple meal, but wholesome, and you are most welcome?" I declined respectfully, but in truth, I would gladly have eaten with them. "I have some food, thank you," I replied motioning towards the brown paper bag that I had been wishing would get lost. While they were busy eating, I pulled out the first package my hand touched in the bag and unwrapped it. I was struck motionless for a moment or two, ham sandwiches, of all things to pull out in the presence of two Muslims in the middle of their meal and just having said their prayers. I decided to brazen it out, they wouldn't recognise it anyway. "What the eye doesn't see the heart doesn't feel," I thought. I don't know what these strict Muslim frontier men would have done if they had known. I ate one sandwich, rolled the other up in paper and put it back in the bag; I didn't even explore the remaining contents. I took out a Mars Bar – one of a dozen – from my small pack and ate that – they were still eating and it smelled delicious.

The train rumbled on slowly for the next two or three hours while I read a western paperback, 'Fighting Caravans' by Zane Grey specially packed for the journey. I didn't appreciate the irony of this until later. Apart from reading, smacking down the mosquitoes, looking out into the blackness of the night, and having a cigarette or two there was little else to do.

When my two companions looked as though they were getting ready for bed, I too got undressed, folded my khaki uniform in the hope of preserving some of the creases, and lay down switching off the light on my side of the compartment. "Good night sahib." "Good night," I said turning to face them. One was lying down full length covered with a thin white cotton sheet, the other, nearer to me, was sitting up on his bunk with his back to the wall of the carriage and his legs drawn up, and his pistol withdrawn from its holster and resting on his stomach.

The day had been full of puzzles, and here was one more for which I had no answer. "Were they expecting trouble? Can't be," I thought. One keeping guard while the other sleeps – maybe. I turned on my side, pulling my small pack a bit closer to me on the bunk where I could get at it easily.

I had a thousand and one thoughts going through my mind, but the clickety click of the wheels on the rails and the buzzing of the fan soon lulled me off to sleep.

Chapter 6

The Train

THE SCHEDULES for meal stops routinely issued by the RTO (Railway Transportation Officer) for long journeys did not, at the best of times, bear much relation to the actual journey. Troop trains were now the lowest priority and were the target for every station master who wanted to keep his section of the line clear for the express and mail trains. It was not unusual for the troopers to be directed on to a loop line or held up for hours in sidings whilst some crack express was given the all clear.

In spite of this knowledge, I was surprised the following morning, when I was woken by the refreshment room bearer offering breakfast on a tray, that we had only covered some one hundred and fifty miles since leaving Calcutta. "Where are we?" I asked, taking the tray from the bearer. "Asensol sahib." I paid him for the breakfast. "Only twenty minutes stop sahib, down line passenger train expected and then you will move off. Tray will be collected at the next stop," he said, as he left the compartment, balancing two or three breakfast trays on each hand with the dexterity of a juggler.

The breakfast was welcome. Scotch porridge oats, two boiled eggs, toast, butter, marmalade and a pot of tea. Every piece of the gleaming white crockery was embossed with the familiar EIR (East Indian Railway) motif and the whole package set on a brilliantly white tray cloth. I sat cross legged on the bunk and ate my breakfast while my two travelling companions dunked their doughnut type bread in steaming hot mugs of tea. It was still only 7:30 a.m. but the sun was well up. There was plenty of hustle and bustle on the opposite platform, presumably travellers awaiting the expected passenger train, and on the track the inevitable crows, mynah birds and sparrows competing for scraps of food. Each one was squawking or tweeting his claim to the territory, and hurriedly flying off to some secluded spot to consume whatever little morsel he had won. Breakfast was eaten and the tray stowed under the bunk for collection at the next stop, whenever that would be. The system of ordering meals was quite efficient. An order would be taken at one station and telephoned down the line, possibly 200-300 miles, the passenger identified by the carriage and bunk number.

Of course, the privilege only applied to first and second class passengers, third class travellers would normally purchase their meals served in disposable earthenware or on huge banyan or plantain leaves from the several platform vendors.

The mobile station barber was allowed to perform with his razor and could complete a shave with just a dozen deft strokes. The whole operation from lathering my chin to handing me a steaming hot towel to wipe off the surplus soap was less than three minutes. I was glad to have been able to avoid this early morning chore as it entailed delving into the depths of my pack to find shaving tackle. I was soon fully dressed and sitting on the bunk when the expected passenger train pulled in on the adjacent track, cutting out the view of the platform and the jostling crowds of would be passengers. It had hardly come to a halt when a shrill whistle blast and a judder or two from our train let us know we were on the move again.

Asensol town was important only as a railway junction, with a major branch line going North East into Assam. During the war it had been a huge supply depot for the American forces with some six to eight thousand Ordnance and Quartermaster Corps personnel engaged in the storage and distribution of war material. By August 1947 it had reverted to a sleepy railway town minus a few of the eligible girls who were lucky enough to leave as American war brides. Many more were left behind with promises and broken hearts. And some with a bit more.

We seemed to be travelling faster now and most of the morning was spent watching the lush fields and tiny villages flashing by through the glass shuttered windows. My companions were sullen, exchanging only a few words between themselves. I read a couple of chapters of my paperback, ate a couple of oranges to quench my thirst, swatted a few flies and read a bit more, while the temperature in the compartment was only a few degrees lower than the sweltering 104 degrees outside. The train rattled on hour after hour with the monotony being shattered periodically by a deafening roar as a train passed by going in the opposite direction.

I once again consulted the schedule of stops provided by the RTO and estimated that we would have a midday stop at Dhanbad. This proved to be correct, as about an hour later, the train slowed to a crawl with the irregular dull clack clack as we crossed from one track to another and slowly drew to a squeaky halt in a siding. We were opposite the main station with four tracks and fifty yards between our train and the platforms on one side, and on my side, a well used footpath bordered by a jungle of weeds and well littered with the recognisable rubbish of a thousand troop trains that had been compelled to spend a few hours there.

My two companions scrambled down on to the track and within a few minutes, the troops were pouring out of the carriages, mess tins at the ready. Two orderly lines soon formed which gradually moved to the rear of the train where the mobile cookhouse was located.

Soon, those that had been first in the queue, were returning to their carriages with mess tins full of steaming hot curry, a mug of tea and chapattis or naan bread. The VCOs and two or three of the British subalterns, walked up and down the lines maintaining order. Once again, I was able to estimate the number of souls on that train and came to the conclusion that there were between one thousand and twelve hundred of all ranks.

I got down from the carriage, passed through the two lines of sepoys and started to walk towards the rear of the train to stretch my legs, as I had spent all morning sitting on my bunk. I watched the activity at the cookhouse for a few minutes, where the regimental cooks were ladling out the curry and lentils from enormous diksees (cooking pots) and handing out the naan bread to the sepoys, who eagerly held out their mess tins to be served. Quite an operation I thought, preparing food for one thousand men in a sixty foot long railcar. I passed the time of day with one of the subalterns, who seemed surprised to see me. He enquired where I was going, and how it came about that I was on a train presumably reserved for his regiment. The briefest of explanations and a casual glance at my travel documents seemed to satisfy his curiosity. Just at that moment I caught sight of three white coated bearers coming across the tracks at the double. "Lunch sahib?" "What have you got?" I responded. He rattled off half a dozen choices, and I settled for the kofta curry and rice, water melon, lime juice and four oranges. The smell of pungent curry was heavy on the air from the cookhouse and I was sure if

I ordered anything else it would be too long in coming. I gave him directions to the carriage and he doubled off having taken orders from the officers in the first class compartment.

"Plenty time sahib, long time standing." From this I gathered we were going to have a long wait in the siding. It was hot out in the sun so I retreated to the comparative cool of the carriage where the fans kept the air circulating, and there were fewer flies to torment you. The lunch duly arrived and like my companions I sat cross legged on my bunk and enjoyed my curry.

There is no curry like that which comes out of an Indian railways dining room, prepared by Goanese cooks and served with all the "sambals" and Bengal pickle (aubergine). Even the most discerning of peppery old colonels would be hard pressed to find fault. The lunch and breakfast dishes cleared away, I settled down to read the "Statesman" which I had ordered with my lunch.

The news of the 18th August was fully occupied with the great celebrations of Independence Day, the selection of ministers for the Government of India, and a column or two of the local communal trouble in Calcutta. There was only an inch or two about communal violence further north in the United Provinces or Punjab. The true situation had either not percolated back to the printing press in Calcutta, or a more likely explanation was that news was deliberately being suppressed by Delhi to avoid spreading panic amongst the minority groups. That was the last newspaper I was to see for a couple of weeks. The heat of the afternoon, coupled with a heavy meal, an ice cold beer and the buzzing of the fans lulled me off to sleep before I got to page four of the paper.

I was shaken into consciousness by a shrill whistle and the jolting of the train as we moved off from the siding at Dhanbad. I instinctively looked at my watch: 17:30 hours. We had been there some four hours. It was still broad daylight, very hot and I was pleased to be on the move again. The batteries on the carriage had run down and the fans were barely turning. As soon as the train picked up speed and the dynamos were turning, the revolutions of the fans increased making it a little less uncomfortable in that hot box. We had been cooped up in the compartment for twenty four hours already and had not made much progress. "It's going to take three days to get to Lahore at this rate," I thought, There was not much to do except sit and stare out of the window and watch the countryside slip away till the sun started to slip below the horizon. The two subedhars went through the ritual of their evening prayers again while I respectfully sat as still as possible.

About an hour after sunset, the train slowed to walking pace and a deep rumbling sound told me that we were on the massive bridge that crosses the Ganges River.

The bridge was desperately in need of major repairs, having suffered from the exceedingly heavy traffic of the war years. It was not possible to close the bridge to traffic while repairs were carried out as it was the only railway bridge across the Ganges for hundreds of miles up and down stream. The river was in full spate, swollen with the monsoon rain from the Himalayas, and was about a mile wide at this time of the year, and flooded the land on both sides of its normal course. The construction of the bridge speaks volumes for the engineers of the day. The massive pillars of the bridge were subjected to tremendous pressure from the huge volume of water during the wet season. In the winter and early summer, the flow dwindled to a comparative trickle, only a little wider than the Thames at London Bridge. The foundations of the pillars went down some two hundred feet through the soft alluvial deposits and rose some sixty feet above high water mark. Huge steel girders made up the spans between pillars, and all this was constructed long before the days of mechanical excavators: every cubic foot of earth dug by hand and moved in baskets balanced on the heads of tens of thousands of women.

The Ganges (Ganga), besides being the holiest river for the Hindus with its origins high up in the Himalayan mountains, was also an exceedingly busy waterway and provided year round irrigation water for the bounteous farming areas on both sides of the river, known as the Gangetic plain.

Benares, the holiest of cities, and the next stop on the bank of the river, was an important city not only from the religious aspect, but also as the commercial centre of the silk weaving trade and world famous for brass and silverware. Benares was the only crossing point for both road and rail for hundreds of miles on either side. All other crossings were made by boat or pontoon type ferry boats for vehicles.

As the train crawled slowly over the bridge, the gangs of repair workmen could be seen clearly in the floodlights, standing on their precarious catwalks with the dark swirling water some sixty feet below. Having cleared the bridge, the train picked up a little speed but within minutes was slowing again to stop at Benares station. We were given the privilege of a remote platform for this stop, and although it was deserted when we came to a halt, it was soon busy with the station vendors who hurriedly crossed the tracks carrying their flat tray like baskets on their heads. They quickly set up their stalls doing a brisk trade with the troops. The platform was poorly lit, but each vendor had his own oil lamp to display his wares and the shadowy figures of the sepoys could be seen milling around in the flickering flames of the lamps.

My two fellow travellers alighted on to the platform and I followed in order to stretch my legs after the long period of confinement. The air was still hot and sultry, the smell of coal smoke from the engine seemed to predominate over all others, the variety of which can only be experienced in India. I did not have the stomach for another heavy meal, but I was not averse to taking my half pint enamel mug, (army issue and still in use as shaving mug sixty years later), to the cookhouse for a steaming hot, very sweet cup of tea.

I gently ambled up and down near my compartment sipping the tea which seemed reluctant to cool down. The mosquitoes, gnats and moths had now formed little whirring clouds attracted by the shadowy illumination of the vendor's lamps, with the occasional bat swooping in low to snatch a victim. The pariah dogs nervously moved about the platform, tails between their legs, sniffing every piece of trash on the floor in the hope of finding a discarded morsel of food. The inevitable little urchins moving from group to group with palms outstretched.

"No mama, no papa baksheesh sahib," pleaded one such urchin, holding up his ragged shirt to show his distended stomach which even he knew was evidence of his hunger and malnutrition. Some would persist long enough to break your heart, periodically bending down to touch your shoes, a gesture of total subjugation. It was not practical to give to all, but the begging look in a little girl's dewy eyes compelled you to fumble in your pocket for a few annas, if for no other reason, than that she would move on and you would not have to look at that pathetic little figure with dark pleading eyes, running nose, tangled matted hair, and rags that passed for clothes.

It was now 21:00 hours, only a few small groups of sepoys stood on the platform, which now seemed even darker as the vendors had left taking their flickering lamps with them. Even the dogs and urchins disappeared into the same darkness to continue their searching and begging as the next train pulled in.

Not being too eager to return to the compartment which was still hot and humid, and no doubt full of mosquitoes, I wandered up the train towards the first locomotive, only one coach away. I was hoping to get some information from the driver as to how long it would be before we moved off. "Any minute now," he said, "Waiting for the six down to pull in, she's standing at the distant signal." He offered, and I accepted another mug of tea, well stewed, off the hob by the fire box.

I gathered he had come down from Delhi the previous day. Benares was the southern end of his territory, and he was returning to base with this train. "Little bit of trouble in the bazaar area in Delhi." Trouble always meant communal fighting, but still no hint of the serious situation that existed further north, and we were heading straight into it.

He was not too talkative and I was tired, so mug in hand I slowly walked back to my compartment. I barely got level with the door when the 'six down' rumbled into the next platform. An ear splitting whistle, a judder or two and we were moving.

My companions were already spreading their bedding rolls in preparation for our second night on board, while I stood at the door, shutters down, watching the lights of Benares city fading in the distance until there was just a halo of light remaining in the clear sky to indicate the presence of the city.

I crossed the compartment to my bunk to sit and stare out of the window into the darkness, still sipping at my mug of tea, which was too hot to drink.

We were moving fairly fast now, and from the clouds of black smoke rushing past the window, and the dull red glow just ahead, I gathered that the stoker had the fire box open and was shovelling on the coal. White hot embers were bouncing along the side of the track leaving a shower of sparks flying in all directions. Then suddenly the red glow disappeared, the fire box was closed, the night looked blacker than ever, and the smell of coal dust was heavy.

I made up my bed and stretched out. Both the subedhars were reading from books which they had carefully unwrapped from brilliantly white muslin cloth. They were like all dutiful Muslims reading a daily passage from the Koran. I felt humbled as the best I could do was the well thumbed paperback. I couldn't concentrate on what I was reading; my thoughts kept bouncing back and forth from the events of the last couple of days to what the future might hold for me in Kuwait. In my mind's eye I could see Jenny standing on the footpath, tears streaming down her face, and within seconds the houseboy bursting his lungs on the platform at Calcutta, beckoning me to get off the train.

The blackness of the night outside was only interrupted by the occasional green light as we rushed through a dimly lit village station or a twinkling light in the distance. Sleep was not going to come easily this night as I had already slept away most of the afternoon after that heavy meal.

Taking another look at the RTOs timetable – Allahabad, Cawnpoore, Alighar, Delhi: the ETAs didn't mean a thing. We were already running well behind schedule. With a spot of luck we could keep moving through the night without interruption and make Delhi some five hundred miles further north, by midday on the 19th August.

My two companions had changed bunks, one was in the prone position and the other had taken up the same position as his brother officer the night before: his pistol close to hand, facing both doors as though expecting someone to try and break in. I wanted to ask him if he was expecting trouble, but dismissed it from my mind, as if, on second thoughts, it was far too delicate a subject. I propped my head up on my pillow, stretched out a bit, picked up my book again and had an unobserved feel for my pistol at the top of my pack. If there was going to be 'trouble' I wanted to make sure I had a chance to defend myself, but I had no idea what form the trouble might take or when or where it would occur.

I read till way past midnight, periodically turning from one side to the other until once again I was overcome by sleep. I must have slept for a couple of hours and wakened to find the compartment in semi darkness. The main lights were off and the one emergency light (permanently on) shrouded in a cotton towel, which only permitted the very minimum of light. After a few moments, my eyes became accustomed to the poor light, and I observed the subedhar on the centre bunk still sitting upright and wide awake. It was about four hours since we had left Benares and it seemed he had not relaxed his vigilance at all during that long period.

The train was rattling along at a fair speed but I had no idea where we were or how far we had progressed. I tried to see what time it was but it was too dark. "It's three o'clock sahib," said the subedhar dangling a big pocket watch. "We have passed Allahabad without stopping and we should be getting to Cawnpore soon, as we have been travelling very fast." I got off the bunk to stretch my legs and stood by the door on my side of the carriage having a cigarette and watching the night flashing by through the glass shutter. It was hot and sticky. I felt grimy from the coal dust, which gets in everywhere. I finished my cigarette and took my pack into the toilet to have a freshen up. I lowered the big heavy foldaway stainless steel basin to the horizontal position, and pressed the knob on the only tap. The water gushed out in spurts, almost too hot from being exposed to the sun all day in the water tank located somewhere in the roof of the carriage.

I felt better after a wash and the colour of the water in the basin and the tell tale marks on the towel let me know that I had every right to feel grimy and dirty. "I'll be glad to get home and get a bath," I thought, but home was still a long way away. As I was packing my towel and soap away I saw bright lights flashing past the glazed window of the toilet and the train began to slow down. I came out of the toilet and found both my companions sitting up. The towel had been removed from the emergency light and all the wooden shutters had been raised, including the ones on my side, so that no one could look in, nor could we see out. "It looks a big city sahib, it must be Cawnpore." The train took a long time to come to a stop, clattering from one set of points to the next. Once again we were on a deserted platform, dimly lit, some two hundred yards away from the main station.

The train had been stationary for some four or five minutes before one of the subedhars lowered one wooden shutter and looked out of the window and up and down the train as though he was looking for something or someone. Both of them were holding their pistols at the ready. "Would you like some charay sahib?" "Yes please," I said, wondering where he was going to get tea at this hour of the morning. He took my mug, opened the door of the carriage, again glancing up and down the train, before replacing his pistol in the holster and alighting on to the platform. He was back again in a few minutes with steaming hot tea. "Always tea in the cookhouse," he said in his own language and I was glad he had the authority to keep the cook sergeant on his toes.

After a while I went down on to the platform to get some air. There were one or two stragglers wandering up to the cookhouse for tea, otherwise the platform was deserted. As I stood under the platform oil lamp with its usual cloud of frenzied nocturnal insects, I noticed a lone unidentifiable figure approaching across the tracks. I didn't take much notice but as I turned away, I heard a voice behind me say, "Any spare bunks in your compartment mate?" I was surprised, to say the least, to hear an Englishman's voice at that hour of the morning. I turned to see a figure in a white shirt, khaki slacks with a kit bag on one shoulder, and a small pack hanging from the other. I was so surprised, I had not had time to answer his question, as he put down his kit bag and pack. "I missed my train going north about six hours ago and the RTO said this trooper may have a spare bunk." By this time I had recovered from the mild shock and realised I was looking at an Englishman about thirty years of age, well tanned, not too tall but powerfully built.

"This is a military train," I said, not too sure that he was entitled to travel on it, although he had mentioned the RTO. "I've got my AB64 Part I here" he offered digging into his rear hip pocket." "Nothing to do with me," was my non-committal reply. "If the RTO says its okay, then it's ok with me." However I was suspicious of this character who knew full well that uniform was obligatory for travelling on a troop train; he had no headdress or any other indication of rank or regiment. "There is a spare bunk," and as I indicated the compartment, he heaved his kit bag up on his shoulder as if it was filled with air and followed me to the carriage.

"This man missed his train," I explained to the subedhars, who made no reply. I pointed to the empty bunk above mine. Up went the kit bag and small pack and, with the agility of a monkey, he swung himself up on to the bunk. "Thanks mate," he said, and with no further explanation or identification, he lay down on the bare bunk, using his pack as a pillow. He seemed to fall asleep almost immediately.

I closed the carriage door, put the wooden shutter up and lay on my bunk. I had given up the pretence of trying to keep the creases in my uniform, the travelling had already put it into such a state, and my houseboy would have been ashamed of me. I lay smoking and thinking, trying to grapple with the jigsaw of events from which I could not create a lucid picture. There was no movement outside we were still stationary. The subedhars had changed places and the other one was on guard again, pistol ever near at hand.

The first grey of the dawn was showing on the sky line, when without warning the train shuddered into motion with a clanging and banging of buffers between the carriages. That was enough to wake the dead at that hour, and then, as an afterthought, a feeble blast on the whistle, which sounded as though even the engine was tired of this interminable journey.

Within an hour, the sun was up and the train rattled along at a fair speed. The landscape had changed quite dramatically. The lush paddy fields and palm trees had been left far behind and had given way to sugar cane fields, huge plots of vegetables and pulses of a dozen varieties. The atmosphere was less humid and the soils drier, clouds of dust were easily raised by the bullock carts on the tracks between the fields, where the farmers were harvesting their produce for market. The occasional flashing glint of sunlight on water gave the location of a Persian wheel with its endless chain of buckets bringing water up from a deep well, the motive power supplied by two or three blindfolded bullocks pulling on a circular track around the well.

It was going to be another long hot dry day. "Could do with a mug of tea," I thought, but had to make do with a couple of mandarin oranges to clear the dust from my throat. It was way past midday before the body above me moved and after a while decided to come down and sit on the bunk beside me. He volunteered the information that he had taken his discharge from his regiment and was on his way to Rawalpindi to marry a 'railway girl' whom he had met while his regiment was posted there. "Just call me Bert," he said and gave me no further information about himself.

It was not unheard of for British soldiers to take their discharge in India, but COs usually put every obstacle in the way, in the hope of dissuading such applicants. The Regimental Padre invariably had a say in the matter, investigating where he could, the background of the girl and family. In this particular case, it seems, in spite of the political situation, Bert had managed to convince every one of his good intentions and had had his way. I didn't quite believe his story, except the part about his girlfriend in 'Pindi, as he seemed to know the town quite well. I had also spent two or three years there while my father was District Magistrate.

It was three o'clock in the afternoon when the train slowed to pull into Alighar Station. We stood at a little used platform while the troops formed their orderly lines for the cookhouse car. The vendors did little trade except for fruit and freshly cut sugarcane, ice cold from a zinc bath full of crushed ice. I was hungry too, and as we were assured by the bearer from the second class waiting room that there was plenty of time, I crossed one set of tracks to the next platform where the restaurant was located. Bert tagged along with me and from the way he enjoyed his mutton curry for breakfast, I gathered he had not eaten for quite some time and that he must have spent a few years in India to have eaten with such relish. When we came out of the waiting room, the last of the troops were being served with their meal. Two or three of the subalterns had eaten in the first class dining room and were crossing the tracks at the same time.

During the afternoon, the train moved forward a couple of hundred yards and we took on coal and water from an overhead hose and gantry Some of the troops alighted, stripped to a loin cloth and took a communal shower under the gushing water hose, right there at the side of the railway tracks. I was in two minds whether to join them or not, as it was so hot and I felt more than grimy. However only twenty or so sepoys managed to avail themselves of this track-side luxury before they were ushered back to their carriages under the orders of their havildhars (sergeants): the one who opened the stopcock received the sharp end of the sergeant's tongue and while he stood rigidly to attention, the cool globules of water trickled down his body. He probably thought it was worth the telling off to feel cool and refreshed.

While we stood in the siding, three or four passenger trains came in and went out, but we were some distance away from the main platforms and this prevented communication between civilian passengers and troops. There was no hint of trouble or panic on the main platform where we had had lunch. The bearers in the waiting rooms were normally a good source of information, but they had little to say except that we could get dinner at Delhi that night. Bert and I spent the remainder of the afternoon sitting on the bunk exchanging information about ourselves and our plans for the future.

He had joined the Lancashire Fusiliers as a boy soldier in 1934, was sent out to North Africa 1942 and India in 1944. He had been there ever since. He had no immediate family, having been raised by an aunt, he had no recollection of mother or father, and felt no great pull to return to England, as he had no home to go to, having lost contact with his foster parents. His prospective father-in-law apparently had some 'pull' on the railways at 'Pindi and had promised to get him a job as soon as he got there.

The sun was starting to drop on the horizon for a third night, a huge ball glowing red which promised another scorching day to follow. The sepoys were now alighting from the train, each one spreading his prayer mat or cloth on the platform removing his shoes and covering his head in a finely crocheted skull cap.

Nothing seemed to distract them and you could not help but admire them for their faith in Islam and the public demonstration of their beliefs. I hope that they had made their peace with Allah, as most of them were not destined to see the next sun rise.

Chapter 7

The Ambush

WITH THE fan barely turning and the light so feeble, you could hardly see across the compartment. The night outside was as black as pitch and there was not a whisper of a breeze. I was relieved to hear the shrill whistle and feel the judder of the train getting into motion. It was about 19:00 hrs when we pulled out of that siding at Alighar and according to the bearer in the waiting room we should get to Delhi about 22:00 hrs. The train picked up speed, the lights got brighter and the fan was thankfully buzzing at full revolutions. There was little to do except sit and look out of the window (glass shutter up) at the darkness seeking the occasional twinkling lights of the villages, or the green light of a signal as it flashed by the window. We were now travelling very fast for a heavily loaded trooper and if we could keep it up without being side tracked we could make Delhi at a reasonable hour and get a light meal.

A heavy rumbling broke into my thoughts and I realised we were crossing the Jumna River (Jumuna) in full flood: the swirling muddy river could be seen as it hurriedly flowed down to link up with the Ganges at Allahabad, where it lost its identity as a tributary of the mighty sacred river.

The hours slipped by, 9 o'clock, 10 o'clock and 11 o'clock and no sign of Delhi coming up, and no slackening of speed. We passed through two or three fairly big stations but did not stop. At the last one we passed through, the train slowed sufficiently for the subedhar to lower the window and shout out to a vendor on the platform. I did not understand what he said or hear the reply. The train cleared the platform and immediately picked up speed again.

The subedhar turned to me after closing the wooden shutter, "We will not go to Delhi sahib." "Why not?" I asked, "Delhi is on the RTO list." "We have been put on a loop line to avoid the heavy mainline traffic." I was not familiar with the loop line and had no idea how many miles or hours it would add to the journey, or even the towns we would pass through.

There was nothing else to do but turn in for the night. The subedhars took up their positions, one lay down to sleep, the other sitting in the 'on guard' position of the two previous nights. Bert swung himself up on to his bunk. I rolled out my bedding and lay down having removed my shoes. One of the subedhars turned out the main lights, leaving only the emergency light which he again covered with a light cotton towel. In this semi darkness, too tired to reason why, or even caring very much I fell off to sleep for the third night on the train.

It did not seem long but must have been a couple of hours, when I awoke to find the train stationary. One of the subedhars was looking out of the window on his side of the train, he crossed the compartment, pistol in hand, lowered the louvered shutter on the opposite door and looked out of the window up and down the train. I sat up and he saw me move in the half light. "No station sahib," he said. I lowered my own shutters and looked up and down the train, no station or platform. There was some heavy hammering coming from immediately behind our carriage and a few seconds later a man stepped out from between the carriages waving an oil lantern.

Without any warning the train jolted forward, I glanced up the train saw nothing unusual, looked back again but the shadowy figure with lantern had disappeared in the darkness, he must have extinguished the lamp he was carrying. I gave it no further thought. I put my shutters up, the subedhar stood by the door, with the shutters down, for a further minute or two, till the train had picked up speed again, he then put his shutters up. "Did you see those men on the track?" he said to me in a subdued voice as if not to waken the other two in the compartment. "I only saw one man on this side; he had a lantern, but only for a few seconds." I said. "There were three or four of them," he insisted and seemed quite agitated.

"They may be dacoits trying to rob the British officers," he said. "The officers are armed and would not hesitate to shoot if someone tried to break into their compartment," I tried to reassure him.

He took up his position on the centre bunk again and I lay back wide awake. The other two, Bert and the other subedhar, had not stirred during the little episode. I could not read my watch in the semi darkness and enquired the time from the alert subedhar. "Two thirty a.m," he replied, pulling out his huge pocket watch as if only to confirm what he had said. The train seemed to be travelling faster than ever. Now that I was fully awake it did seem strange that the train should stop in the middle of nowhere at that hour of the morning. "For how long did we stop at that spot?" I asked him. "Only two or three minutes," he said. I was not sure if the stop had been longer or I had woken just as the train stopped.

I lit a cigarette and was lying back with my eyes closed trying to figure out what the subedhar was so agitated about. No dacoits (robbers) would be so foolhardy as to try to rob a military train, and furthermore why would they advertise their presence with all that hammering, the waving of the lantern, hardly likely that two engine drivers would be co-conspirators. I concluded that they were a gang of railway workers tapping the lines for cracks or loose fish plates, and that the subedhar was letting his imagination run away with him.

The train rattled on for another hour and in spite of another cigarette or two I could not get off to sleep again. The subedhar had in the last hour lowered and raised the louvered shutters on both sides of the carriage and looked out two or three times. I had no idea what he was looking for or what he expected to see. "Sahib I am very worried and frightened for you and the other sahib." He suddenly came out with the remark at the same time wakening the other subedhar.

They spoke for half a minute and the one who had just been roused went to the door of the carriage, lowered the shutter and lent out as far as he could. "We have lost part of the train and all our officers have gone." I sat bolt upright, "See for yourself." He beckoned me to the open shutter. I lent out to take a look. I felt a cold shiver and broke out in a damp sweat. We had indeed 'lost' all the carriages and wagons immediately linked to our carriage and this included the first class compartment with all the British officers. It immediately came home to me that the activity on the line an hour earlier was someone disconnecting those carriages from the remainder of the train. "Why?" I said to myself, but no answers came to me.

While standing at the door with the shutter down I noticed a motor vehicle with headlights on about one hundred yards away. We were at a point where the road and rail track ran almost parallel and no more than one hundred or one hundred and twenty yards separated them. One of the subedhars joined me at the window and we looked up the right hand side of the train, which had started to slow down, and we saw more vehicles on the road all stationary and they seemed to be about fifty yards apart. "If trouble starts you must get off the train and run for your life," he said, jerking me in from the window quite violently. The train was still moving at a fast run. "Get your shoes on, wake the other sahib." He barked out his order as if assuming command. I crossed to my bunk, woke Bert and told him to get his shoes on while groping for mine in the semi darkness. The train was slowing. Bert got up, "I've got my shoes on," he said and I finished tying my laces.

Both subedhars were standing and peering out from half lowered shutters on the right hand side of the compartment, pistols in hand. I pulled my small pack nearer to me, removed my pistol, put the spare magazine in my left hand breast pocket and stuck the pistol in the waist band of my trousers. Bert was sitting on the top bunk, legs dangling just above my shoulders. The train was still moving. I heard crackling like fireworks on Chinese New Year's Eve, and instantly the compartment erupted into a shower of splinters of wood, metal fragments and glass. "Get down," one of the subedhars shouted. I needed no second warning. I lay flat on the floor as close to my steel trunk as I could get, knees pulled up, my face touching the floor, I could smell the coal dust. Bert just tumbled off the top bunk. The train was still moving slowly. Another shower of glass, wood splinters, jagged pieces of nickel flew about, from bullets which fragmented after striking metalwork in the compartment.

"Bren guns," I thought, as I cautiously peeped over the top of my steel trunk just in time to see one of the subedhars take a full burst of eight or ten rounds in the chest. He was flung across the centre bunk, his head hanging back over the edge. He made one movement as though to get up and fell back, dead. The firing continued unabated for another two minutes and, I estimated from the crackling, that there were at least six to eight Bren guns putting in a continuous, concentrated fire. Every few seconds there was the ripping sound of slugs striking our compartment causing a fresh shower of wood and glass splinters.

I could hear the bullets penetrating my steel trunk on the other side, fortunately they had lost most of their momentum in passing through the heavy bodywork of the coach, upholstery and solid teak wood of the lower bunks, for I would surely have been riddled.

The train stopped. "Run sahib," the voice sounded pleading. I raised my head for a second but was down again in a flash as a fresh burst hit the compartment. Bert was struggling in the semi darkness to untangle the dead subedhar's lanyard and pistol. "Get ready to run as soon as the firing stops," shouted Bert. He pulled himself across the floor to the door on the left side of the carriage and started to struggle to pull the heavy door open while still in the prone position.

Another burst of fire, and now rifle shots were coming over in twos and threes. The rifle fire had been drowned out by the Brens. The emergency lights were still on. Two or three rifle shots were coming in every few seconds, then a lull and everything was quiet after the pandemonium, except for a lot of shouting in the distance.

"Go now sahib, I must stay with my men, go now," he repeated urgently. I half raised myself to crawl on all fours towards the door which Bert was still struggling to open. The subedhar was sitting up on the floor half leaning on the bunk. I moved towards the door, squeezing past the dead subedhar whose body had half slipped into the space between the bunks, his head touching the floor and almost blocking my way. A pool of blood had collected on the floor, I crawled through the warm sticky mess, my hands and knees tacky, my khaki slacks absorbing the blood like blotting paper. I saw his face in the half light, eyes open, staring blankly at the ceiling.

I looked back at the other subedhar who was now almost upright. "Thank you," I said, but I'm sure he didn't hear me, for as I spoke, I saw the muzzle of a shot gun slide over the bottom of the now shattered window. With a deafening blast and a flash which illuminated the compartment for a second I saw his head jerk back almost severed from his body. He took the full blast, at point blank range, in the throat and neck; I felt the warm blood splatter over my face and arms. He fell back in a lifeless heap, the ceiling of the compartment was dripping with blood and trickling down the wall at the rear of the compartment. I was frightened.

Seconds later, I saw a white turban rise above the shattered window of the door, a black bearded face and shoulders appeared and he was levelling the shot gun to fire at Bert, who was fully exposed on the floor, having got the door open. I heard the cocking action of the shot gun as he pulled back the hammer. My action was instinctive.

"Never point a gun at anyone," my father had instructed me as a youngster, "unless you intend to kill him." The thought went through my mind a thousand times faster than it took to write. I did not aim; I pointed my pistol at the white turban, from my unseen position between the bunks. I fired; "A pathetic little crack," I thought, compared to the terrible blast of the shot gun which followed half a second later, blowing a hole as big as a plate in the ceiling above Bert. I did not see the strike, but the turban and bearded face disappeared from the window frame. He must have pulled the trigger as a reflex action as he fell back to the track.

"Let's go," I shouted. Bert dived out of the compartment into the darkness; I followed using the three steps of the carriage dragging my pack with one hand, and with a pistol in the other.

We slipped, tumbled, slid and rolled down the steep thirty foot embankment in the darkness with the train above us. At the bottom we were confronted by an almost solid wall of tinder dry tiger grass (surpath) ten feet tall growing in clumps with every long blade as sharp as a razor. We hurriedly pushed our way through this curtain, quite oblivious to the searing, slashing cuts being inflicted to face and arms. We were aware of a terrified shouting and screaming and occasional shots coming from the direction of the train now some thirty feet above us, and thirty yards behind us.

We pushed our way about fifty yards into this tangled mass; I was using my pack at face height to afford some protection from the lacerating blades. We did not need to speak as every step revealed our position with the cracking of the dry canes that support the fluffy foxtail type of flower some five or six feet above us. The brushing aside of the long blades of grass sounded like large sheets of newspaper being crumpled, only much louder. The high tension of the last fifteen minutes had left me exhausted and disorientated. "Sit down where you are," said Bert. I couldn't see him, it was pitch black, although no more than four or five paces separated us. The screaming and shouting was fainter now as we were partly screened from the train by the dense growth. We sat there for a few minutes hardly daring to breathe. I took the opportunity of the short break to roll down my shirt sleeves to give me some protection from the grass. "I've been hit," Bert said. "Oh God don't let him die on me," I thought. "I've been hit in the thigh."

In the fever pitch excitement, he had not felt any pain, but here in the dark he could feel the wet sticky patch of blood coming through his khaki trousers, and the warm trickle of blood collecting in his shoe. Like a well trained, battle experienced soldier Bert applied a tourniquet to his thigh, with his leather belt. In the darkness and almost quiet, we could hear the tiger grass rustling and the dry canes cracking about twenty paces to our right.

"We are not alone," I thought. Some others managed to survive that murderous, concentrated fire. I could only think about what was happening now. The events of even only a few minutes previously seemed too remote and required more concentration. The visual flashes in my mind seemed easier to cope with as they kept changing so rapidly; the subedhar taking the full blast of the shot gun, the blood splattered over the ceiling and trickling down the cream painted wall, the black bearded face and white turban framed in the window, these came and went so rapidly, no effort was required.

The quiet was suddenly broken by repeated bursts of a Bren coming from the direction of the train. I lay down as flat as possible, the terrible grass slashing at my neck and hands; the bullets could be heard scything their way through the dry grass. The attackers were firing blindly into the tall grass in the hope of killing those few who had managed to escape. The firing stopped. "Let's move on," said Bert in little more than a whisper.

Bent double and pushing my pack ahead of me for some protection from the grass, the sky behind us was suddenly lit up with a red glow and within minutes the long tongues of flames could be seen leaping wildly thirty feet into the sky. Within a few minutes there was a solid wall of fire behind us, there was little wind fortunately, and we had a lead of thirty or forty yards on the flames. We hurriedly pushed our way forward, the red glow lighting up the wicked grass in front of us. A glance back, revealed a wall of fire with thick clouds of white smoke rushing skywards, sucking in the ash and glowing embers in the upward draught and dropping them again over a wide area about us. It was like a giant fireworks display, the flames shooting into the sky thirty or forty feet and the red hot embers falling out like a waterfall. The train was silhouetted against the skyline glowing red, reflecting the dancing flames.

Bert was making more progress than I was, in spite of his wound, and kept shouting back at me to keep moving. The falling burning embers had reduced our lead on the wall of fire; small outbreaks were starting round us and spreading rapidly. The embers were leapfrogging the fire faster than we could move through the tangle. These fresh outbreaks were all round us now, the dense white smoke was choking, the smell of burning becoming stronger. Suddenly, a wall of flame burst up in front of me, not ten feet away. The intense heat forced me to hold up my pack to shield my face. I moved to the right, to scout around this new obstacle, the cracking of the burning, the rush of air, the grass waving violently in the draught, the suffocating smoke, all combined, to cause a state of confusion. As I stumbled over the clumps, pushing my way through, I came shoulder to shoulder with a sepoy. "Bhago, sahib, bhago," (run) suddenly there were two of them looking for a way around their own wall of fire. The two walls were converging towards one another rapidly closing the gap. It was now or never, I thought as I pushed my way through the tangle. The smoke was choking me, my eyes were streaming and my lungs burning from breathing smoke. Coughing and spluttering, as the two walls of fire became one, I felt myself dragged bodily through the gap, the flames licking at my face, my hair and eyebrows singed, throat and nose dry and smarting from breathing the smoke and hot air. The two sepoys had dragged me through the last remaining escape route. Had they not, I would surely have been incinerated behind that wall of fire. They continued to urge me on as I staggered and stumbled from one clump to the other, the advancing fire only a few feet behind. Another twenty yards of this deadly race between the fire and the three of us and we suddenly burst into the open.

A track, twenty feet wide, was in front of me with two pairs of willing hands pulling me through the last few yards of that terrible heat. The smoke was thick, "Where is the other sahib?" I asked. I got no reply. "Run sahib, run." "Where to?" I thought. The smoke was so thick you could not see what was on the other side of the track, the burning canes were now falling across our pathway, everywhere was lit up by the flames. I crossed the twenty feet of track and heard water splashing, then I caught a glimpse of the water reflecting the flames; an irrigation canal. Without any further hesitation, I jumped in joining the two sepoys. "The other sahib?" I managed to gasp out. "Where is he? Did he get through? He was wounded in the leg."

We moved away from the bank towards the middle of the canal to avoid the heat and falling canes. The water was only three feet deep, a brown muddy colour, and I remember it felt ice cold after the terrible inferno. I wanted to shout out to Bert, and then I nearly fell over him sitting in the water up to his armpits.

The huge flames had died down immediately in front of us. The dry grass had been consumed in the flames within a few minutes leaving the canes standing and burning until they broke and fell to the ground to continue burning. The clumps around the roots were smouldering and smoking, but for a hundred yards on either side, the inferno raged. The undergrowth was still burning fiercely, years of accumulated dead growth revealed a field of glowing red hot flickering embers.

We could see the train now, three hundred yards away standing high on the embankment, the emergency lights still on, and brighter lights beyond, which I took to be the headlights of the vehicles which had illuminated the train as the target. There was still some movement on the train and shouting which came over to us very faintly. I went back to the bank, to retrieve my pack and was surprised to see hundreds of hare and other rodents scurrying up and down the track and two wild spotted deer, heads hanging low as though dejected at the loss of their young; they had all been driven to the safety of the track by that awful raging fire.

We waded across the canal, Bert was limping heavily. None of us had spoken much. We clambered out and within a few paces found ourselves in a huge field of cauliflowers. We lay down between the rows, too exhausted to do more than reflect that we were lucky to be alive. It was now past four o'clock in the morning and in another hour or so the first light of dawn would be showing. I looked around and could see a halo of light in the sky, indicating the presence of a city in a north westerly direction. "We can't stay here too long," I said to Bert. "We are too exposed, besides we will all get sun stroke by midday. We have to have a look at your leg as soon as it gets light."

When the first grey light of dawn began to show I looked across the fields and saw a group of date palms in the distance and I could hear the faint hum of an electric motor coming from the same direction. Bert had difficulty in getting up, the two sepoys helped him up and between them half carried, half dragged him through the fields towards the trees I had indicated. As we approached the trees I could see a crude shelter and the hum of the motor was quite clear. We approached cautiously and found an old man asleep on a charpoy under the shelter, which had been woven from the fallen fronds of the date palms. The rush of water in the irrigation drain was now louder than the motor. We were screened from view on all three sides by maize, and sugar cane fields. We woke the old man who, seeing we were armed, begged for mercy. He probably thought we were all Muslims ready to take revenge; the old man was a Sikh. We assured him his life was not in danger and he seemed relieved when I spoke in my imperfect Urdu. "I'll make you tea," he said as though paying a ransom for his life. "Get on with it," I said as he disappeared into a small hut. While he was boiling water for the tea, I looked at the water in the irrigation drain, it was cool and crystal clear and I discovered was being pumped up from the well by the electric motor.

The two sepoys had put Bert down on the smooth earth floor of the shelter and were removing his trousers. As it got lighter, and I looked at the others, I realised what a sorry sight we were; blood spattered, crumpled and still wet clothes from sitting in the canal, our faces blackened and sore from the smoke and ash of the fire, hair having being burned almost to the roots, and it seemed a thousand cuts from the merciless tiger grass. Bert's leg looked a mess, a deep four inch gash in the back of the thigh, no sign of an entry or exit hole. The sepoys set about washing the wound out with the clear cool water. Bert lay there on his stomach wincing now and again but not complaining. One of the sepoys beckoned me over to where Bert lay and pointed out to me a piece of shiny jagged metal embedded in his flesh, at one end of the gash. "It must come out sahib, or in two days he will die."

There was no mention of a doctor as we all knew it was quite useless to even think of finding one out in the wilderness, or even in the city if we could get there. The bleeding had stopped but the wound was raw and gaping, a wide patch of inflammation was already showing against his white skin. With the minimum of explanation, one sepoy put a piece of wood between Bert's teeth and sat on his back while I held Bert's leg down with my weight. The other sepoy produced his army issue jack knife and with a couple of quick probes in the flesh he levered it out. Bert gave out a scream of pain and within seconds mercifully fainted into oblivion. The piece of nickel was indeed a distorted bullet which had struck metal first, flattening and tearing, then ricocheting across the compartment to bury itself in Bert.

I was now digging in my pack, I was the only one with any possessions if that's what you could call them; I unearthed the last khaki shirt and trousers I had worn in Calcutta, my shaving tackle, a towel, soap, a pair of tennis shoes, army sewing kit (housewife) and two waterproof packs of field dressing (army issue). The sepoy recognised them at once and opened one and applied the sterile pad to the wound and bandaged the leg, while Bert was still recovering from his long faint.

The old man appeared with a diksee full of tea and earthenware cups and a dozen or more corn on the cob, freshly roasted over his fire and smeared with ghee and sprinkled with salt and pepper. Among the other things to come out of my pack were four packs of cigarettes, the brown paper bag containing stale sandwiches (I discarded the ham, but ate the cheese) three or four oranges which I shared around and a couple of mars bars. We all ate and were thankful for the tea, roasted corn cobs and dried dates – very filling and sustaining.

The two sepoys had been questioning the old man who admitted having heard the firing during the night but did not know what it was all about. We also ascertained that, if we followed the railway track, we were four hours walking distance from Ambala city, There would be no workers in the fields that day as nearly all were Muslims; there had been communal trouble in the city and they were afraid to leave the security of their area.

The sun was well up now and I walked around the hut which turned out to be much bigger than I first observed. There were two stables behind the hut with a cow in one and a horse in the other. A two wheeled cart (tum tum) stood in the yard with sundry pieces of harness hanging over the shafts. In another corner there were several agricultural implements and a huge pile of maize cuttings and cabbage or cauliflower leaves, presumably for feeding the animals. Near the well, which was twenty five yards from the hut, there were three fig trees, a mulberry tree, heavily laden with ripening fruit, and affording plenty of shade. We all stripped down to the minimum and bathed in the cool clear water passing the soap around. I was glad to get the dried blood off my arms, hands and knees, the ashes out of my hair and ears. I was fortunate I had a change of clothes. I gave my stained shirt to one of the sepoys who promptly washed all his clothes in the running water and did Bert's khaki trousers at the same time. The clothes were dry within an hour.

Keeping an eye on the old man all the time, we lay down on a carpet of harvested maize stalks in the shade to make plans for our next move. The old man explained he was the chowkidar (watchman) for the pump and had been appointed by the wealthy landowners to irrigate the fields.

For the first time we spoke of the events of the last three days. I had mulled over the three main aspects: first the disarming of the troops at Calcutta, second the disconnecting of six or seven carriages containing the British Officers and third the early morning ambush, and had come to the conclusion that the whole operation had been planned well in advance. The presence of six or eight machine guns and vehicles indicated to me the involvement of the Indian Army, though I never actually saw any military personnel. The houseboy running along the platform telling me to get off the train now began to make sense. He had already heard 'bazaar talk' of what was going to happen and was trying to warn me, another two minutes more and I'm sure he would have told me.

The inordinately long delays to the train, pushed into sidings, allowed plenty of time for military communications and planning to be passed up the line. Yet it seemed inconceivable that senior military officers and possibly ministers of the government could be involved in such a diabolical plan. The attack, to massacre a complete train load of unarmed Muslim troops, could not have been carried out without the collusion of both the military and the government.

The purpose of the removal of the British officers was two fold; first to avoid any possibility of them getting killed, which would have had severe inter-governmental repercussions and would have destroyed the impartiality of the British Army. Secondly the absence of any independent witnesses would not lend credence to any rumours which may have circulated after the event.

As for the motive I can offer no explanation, other than, that the slaughter was planned as nothing more than retaliatory revenge for the Hindus and Sikhs being killed in the North Punjab (now Pakistan).

The horrendous events taking place in the Punjab were not known to the general public at that time, but were known in government and military circles.

The two sepoys appeared to be the only survivors from their carriage which held between sixty to eighty men. There may have been more who managed to get away in the confusion and the darkness. How many perished in that raging inferno of tiger grass no one will ever really know. The vultures and jackals would have destroyed most of the evidence within a couple of days.

Bert and I decided to make for Ambala station at dusk, and the two sepoys had already made up their minds that they were going to stay with us as we afforded the best possibility for their survival. It was not safe to move in broad daylight, as I suspected the army maybe looking for survivors and would mow us down from a distance. We spent the remainder of the morning and part of the afternoon resting under the fig and mulberry trees, keeping an eye on the old man, who was busy in and out of his hut feeding his animals, and generally getting on with his chores.

I could smell cooking, but did not dare to presume the old man was cooking for us. I had already told the old man our intention to get to Ambala station and since it was impossible for Bert to walk there I expected him to take us in his tum tum, and if he didn't agree to take us, we would take his horse and cart anyway.

It was scorching hot even in the shade of the trees. Not a breath of wind could be felt and a million flies tormented us from the heap of cow dung in the yard. We could not see the train from where we were because of the sugar cane fields and although only a thousand yards from the track, we heard no trains passing. The vultures were already circling the train, high in the sky, gliding effortlessly on the thermals, their unerring instincts guiding them to their next meal.

Bert slept most of the day and the sepoys took it in turns to keep an eye on the old man while the other dozed. I lay there turning over in my mind what had occurred since I left Calcutta and what we would do, if and when, we got to Ambala station. I spent an hour lying on my back looking up at a low overhanging branch, watching a four inch long praying mantis perfectly camouflaged against the translucent mulberry leaves, patiently waiting for a caterpillar on an adjacent leaf to eat its way within striking distance.

I knew what was going to happen, the mantis never moved, its huge eyes focussed on its next victim. The caterpillar blissfully unaware of the fate awaiting it, eating rapidly along the edge of the leaf, till, faster than the eye could follow, the mantis struck out with two arms and brought in the victim impaled on needle sharp claws. The sudden movement of the mantis brought me back to reality and the predicament we were in.

I sat up to find one of the sepoys trying to fashion himself a pair of sandals from an old car tyre he had found near the well. He had lost one of his "chapals" while running through the tiger grass. I gave him my tennis shoes, one size too small, but I suggested he cut out the toe caps, he was so pleased and I took the opportunity to thank them both again for saving my life in that dreadful fire.

At about six o'clock, when the sun had lost most of its searing heat, the old man appeared with a diksee full of vegetable buggia (stew) and thick chapattis. We all ate, unceremoniously breaking the chapattis into pieces and dipping into the stew, eating with our fingers. It smelled good, it tasted good, and I was more than satisfied, in spite of the fact that I knew the meal had been cooked over dried cow dung pats, the traditional fuel of the poor.

But then who was I to complain, at that moment I ranked amongst the poorest.

The old man appeared with his cart, the horse already between the shafts. "Its time to go now sahib," he said indicating the sun low in the sky, "In one hour it will be dark and it's a long way to the motor road." The horse looked a sturdy animal, well fed and quite capable of hauling the cart loaded with a ton of cauliflowers. We helped Bert on to the floor of the cart; the old man walked leading the horse down a rough track between the fields, screened on both sides by the tall sugar cane: the two sepoys walked behind. It took half an hour to get to the motor road with Bert and I being bounced around on the cart, holding on to the low sides to prevent ourselves from being thrown off. We crossed the canal by a well constructed low bridge and passed under the railway track and through an archway. The fields came to an end abruptly and tiger grass took over.

One of the sepoys scrambled up the embankment and cautiously looked down the line, he reported that the train was still there but could see no vehicles or human movement. I was tempted to return to the carriage to recover some of my possessions, mainly my camera and collection of photographs, but the thought of the blood drenched compartment and the two dead subedhars deterred me. In any event I knew the train would have been looted by the howling mob which took over after Bert and I had run down that embankment. There would be little chance of finding anything except the terrible cargo of mutilated bodies.

I especially regretted the loss of my camera and photographs as they would have been of great use to anyone preparing an historical record of events of that period. The ever present vultures were now sitting on the roof of the carriages, having gorged themselves to a state where they could hardly fly; the jackals would no doubt carry on the feeding after dark.

A couple of hundred yards more and we were on the macadam road, and looking back I could see the train. The old man and the two sepoys now also got on board the cart and with a few deftly placed whacks with a cane, from the old man, the horse broke into a steady trot.

The first triangular whitewashed obelisk indicated Ambala 7 miles, allowing for his age and a couple of rests along the way the old man's estimate of four hours walk was not too far out. However, I was glad we had not been compelled to put it to the test as we could never have made it with Bert in his condition. It was soon dusk and shortly afterwards it was dark.

We heard no trains and encountered no other movement on the road. A glow in the sky told us we were going in the right direction. A few occasional whacks with the cane kept the horse trotting and before long the first dim street lamps began to show as we approached the outskirts of the city.

The streets were deserted, but lantern lights showed through the open barred windows of the dwellings, we seemed to be surrounded by a deathly silence, except for the muffled clop, clop clop of the horse's hooves as they made contact with the sun softened tarmac. The old man obviously knew his way around the city well and took the short cuts up darkened alleyways, where groups of people were sitting outside their homes on charpoys trying to catch any breath of cool air which may have come their way. Finally he drew up the horse and said he was frightened to go any further because he was getting close to the Muslim area.

The station was not far away now and we could walk there in ten minutes. The two sepoys were sullen as they knew they were in hostile territory and it was possible that the train had been looted and their wounded comrades slaughtered by some of these very people sitting out here in the alleyways, who would no doubt have given them the same treatment if they had suspected the presence of Muslims.

I gave the old man ten rupees for which he offered profuse thanks, and pointing with the cane, indicated the direction of the station and told us to go quickly and not to speak to anyone.

We kept close together and hurried off keeping in the shadows, the sepoys helping Bert, while I nervously fingered my pistol in case we were set upon. Within a couple of hundred yards we came up to a wire fence and beyond the fence lay the railway tracks. We got through the fence and began to walk along the track towards the station platforms which were dimly lit some five hundred yards away. There were goods wagons in the sidings and we walked between the tracks with wagons on both sides, it was dark and we were glad of the protection of the wagons.

About two hundred yards from the platform we came level with a well lit signal box about twenty feet above the track with steps leading up to it. I could see the long bank of levers above window level and at least two Sikh soldiers, rifles slung on their shoulders. One was speaking on a field telephone though we could not hear what was being said.

We kept low in the shadows of the wagons and moved on towards the platforms as quietly as we could. As we reached the end of the wagons, there stood a small shunting engine hissing steam gently, with the stoker raking the fire box, red hot ashes falling to the track. We hurried on in the open as fast as Bert and the darkness would allow and a couple of minutes later heard coal being shovelled, the sound coming from the direction of the shunting engine.

We reached the platform and in the dim lights (only a few were on) coming from high up in the black smoke and soot darkened roof, we were confronted by a sea of bodies squatting on the bare floor with their pathetic bundles pulled up to them. Some were lying full length. The platform on the other side of the track was similarly completely covered in sitting, lolling and prone figures. As my eyes became accustomed to the dim light, and we picked our way between the bodies looking for somewhere to sit down, I became aware that nearly all the people on the platform were women and children. The women in their long white gowns (burkha) were covered from head to foot, nursing babies or trying to comfort older children lying uncomfortably on the stone floor. There was hardly any sound except for the odd cry from a baby somewhere in that mass of heads and bundles all huddled together.

The four of us gingerly picked our way forward till we found ourselves in the main ticket hall, which was just as crowded and quiet except for some activity in one corner. There we found four men wearing green armbands with a crescent moon in white, indicating they were members of the Muslim League, sitting at a table. As we approached they seemed confused to see us and got up to greet us. As our identity became clear, Bert was immediately given a chair to sit on, there was a lot of chatter between the four men and the two sepoys, all too fast for me to fully understand.

We were ushered into a small room where one of the four men joined us, a hurricane lantern lit the room, the man set about lighting a primus stove and a kettle was placed on it. When the frantic agitated conversation slowed down and I could get a word in, I was shocked and stunned by what the man had to say. Communal trouble had broken out almost immediately after Independence Day, there had been hand to hand fighting between Sikhs and Muslims, many hundreds of men, women and children had been killed on both sides. Swords, axes, daggers and spears had been used with the odd shot gun, Muslim property had been set ablaze, mosques desecrated, and much of the Muslim area was completely raised to the ground and looted. Many hundreds were still in the Muslim area of the city, not far away, holed up in a desperate attempt to safeguard their property, in the vain hope that the police or army would separate the battling communities.

What we saw here, at the station, were some of the survivors who were unable to get away because the trains had stopped running two days prior to our arrival. There was no food and water, except from a hand pump in the station yard out front, which could only be used at night, as someone was sniping at anyone who tried to draw water in daylight. Several had been killed. Electricity, water and telephones cut off, the station emergency generator was supplying the power for the lights and was under the control of the few Muslim men around the station complex. Movement outside the main building was dangerous and the sniping had been going on for two days.

We learned that many of the people we had seen on the platforms were already dead and many more were suffering from horrific wounds from which they would surely die within a day or two. The station was virtually under siege. It was now nearing midnight and I was almost completely exhausted from lack of sleep.

We spent the remainder of the night in fitful sleep, slumped in wickerwork chairs from the first class waiting room. The mosquitoes were troublesome and the atmosphere stifling due to lack of ventilation. The incessant chatter of the four officials made sleep almost impossible.

I must have dozed off towards the early hours because I awoke to find one of the sepoys standing over me with two steaming hot mugs of tea for Bert and myself. It was still early morning and after the welcome tea and a quick sponge down, face and hands only, with the corner of the towel and half an enamel jug of water brought in by the second sepoy, it was time to assess the reality of our situation.

The four officials, distinctly bleary eyed and haggard looking, were still sitting at the table in the main hall, which seemed even more crowded than the previous evening. I picked my way through the crowd on the floor out onto Platform No. 1 which was equally crowded, and I could see over a double set of railway tracks to No. 2 Platform and No. 3 and 4 beyond, all completely occupied by a seething mass of humanity but strangely quiet.

The stench was dreadful, the flies were swarming in clouds, the tracks were being used as an open latrine, dead bodies covered in the traditional white shroud and already in an advanced state of putrefaction lay, on the platform. Relatives sat nearby, most too stunned, into a state of shock, to show any form of emotion, placidly sitting, expressionless in a semi trance, awaiting whatever fate Allah had in store for them. Here and there some older men seemed to muster the last reserves of energy to prostrate themselves in prayer as a final gesture of their faith; the remainder had been completely overtaken by despair.

I returned to the main booking hall and sat at the table with the four officials who seemed preoccupied with compiling endless lists of names of new arrivals rather than doing anything practical to alleviate the physical conditions that existed round them. "We must move the dead bodies off the platforms," I said. They looked at me in utter disbelief, as though I was suggesting the impossible. How can this possibly be achieved, there are so many? Where will we put them? There is no transport. Who will move them? The questions came thick and fast.

As I was putting my plan to them there was a commotion outside the main station. The latest victim of the sniping was being brought in from the water pump in the yard. It was a woman who had been foolish enough to think that the "chardah" would deter the snipers, she died within a few minutes having been hit by a single bullet fired from the signal box less than two hundred yards away. One of the sepoys stood over her, his jaw clenched in anger, moving his head from side to side in a gesture of utter frustration.

It was a long scorching hot day with little movement in the hall or on the platforms except for a gang of eight or ten able bodied men with four canvas stretchers, picking up the bodies from Platform No. 1 and moving them to the northern end of the platform. This was the first phase of the plan which the four officials had agonised about, after I had outlined what I intended to do. I had anticipated a reluctance by the relatives to allow the bodies to be taken away, but there was little or no resistance; a whimper here and there as children were taken away from young mothers, too shocked in some cases, to know what was happening, and the old men who did, were in a state of despair.

Over two hundred bodies were laboriously moved to the end of Platform No. 1, from there the gang of men, their mouths and noses covered in the windings of their turbans to filter the stench, moved to Platform No. 2, to continue the operation.

Meanwhile I had been scouting the length of Platform No 1 and found a tool box in a workman's hut with crowbars, axes, shovels, hacksaws, sledge hammers and a miscellany of lifting and cutting equipment normally associated with maintaining railway tracks.

I also discovered to my amazement that the two fire hydrants on Platform No. 1 gushed out dirty brown water under full pressure. With the assistance of the four officials, we rounded up further reluctant helpers to run out the hoses and wash away, down into the sewers, the many days collection of excrement from the shallow drains between each set of railway tracks. The young men rounded up for this most disagreeable task were at first reluctant and hostile at being called upon to carry out such demeaning work, normally the work of the lowest class of 'untouchables'. However, after I had personally manned the nozzle with its powerful jet of water for a few minutes, they took over and seemed to derive some perverse satisfaction in watching the stinking brown sludge disappear through the manhole sized grate into the main sewers.

As the sun started to go down below the horizon I returned to the small room where Bert was still sitting awkwardly in the wicker chair. He seemed more cheerful and was busy eating rice and lentils. I was just about to ask, when one of the officials handed me a similar enamel plate with a shiny spoon (taken from the dining room) piled high with rice and running over with hot bright yellow lentils. I was not about to question my benefactor as to its origin but ate with relish, as I could hardly remember when I had last eaten.

One of the officials explained that food had been brought in from the city and was being distributed to all. The two sepoys, who were also included in the share out, were on their knees praying before touching a morsel. I once again felt deeply humbled at this demonstration of a tremendous unshakeable faith. The meal was followed by the inevitable mug of steaming sickly sweet tea, the first since the early morning.

I suddenly realised I was tired and slumped into the other chair as I had been on my feet all day. Bert and I discussed our plight and how to get out of it. If food could be brought in we should be able to get out the same way, but I was not so sure our situation would be any better in the city; we may be jumping from the frying pan into the fire. Just walking out along the railway track was out of the question with Bert only able to hobble with his game leg.

It was now getting dusk and I remembered the row of hurricane lanterns I had seen hanging in the workman's hut at the end of Platform No. 1. Taking the two sepoys with me, we went to the hut and took three or four of the lanterns and a more than half full, rusty, five-gallon drum of paraffin. I explained to them what I intended to do.

We walked along the track to a siding only thirty yards from the end of Platform No. 1 where a row of empty goods wagons were standing. We uncoupled the first one by the light of the lamp, released the brake lever and using two crowbars between wheels and railway line levered the wagon into motion. One of the sepoys made short work of the lock on the lever with the sledgehammer that allowed us to move the points so that we could join the main track leading to the platform. There was a slight incline and it took us fifteen minutes to position the wagon alongside the bodies that had been placed there during the course of the day. The sepoys were quick to understand the intention, load the bodies onto the wagons and move them as far away from the platform as possible.

The previous forty-eight hours had kept me in almost constant contact with these two fine men. Both six feet tall, broad of shoulder with fine chiselled proud features, full of character, which is common to the men from the Northwest frontier with Afghanistan. I enquired their names and with a military stance of heels together they replied, in proud fashion, Iqbal Ali Khan and Hussein Ali Khan, followed by their regimental numbers. Again I was touched, that even in this awful predicament, these two men could still maintain their military bearing and display the discipline of well trained soldiers; both were wearing among other decorations, the North African Campaign Star.

Hussein volunteered to round up the same men and get them to load the wagons; I left him to get on with this, a most gruesome task. Iqbal the older of the two men, both in their mid thirties, returned with me to the little office, carrying the paraffin drum, while I carried the lanterns and the first aid box which we had removed from the wall of the hut. Having broken off the hasp and staple, as the box was locked; we were surprised to find it well stocked with bandages, lint, gauze and large containers of pungent yellow powder, which I immediately recognised as iodaform and sulphonamide. I promptly went over to Bert to apply a fresh dressing with a liberal sprinkling of the yellow powder. The wound was clean, very tender, but healthier looking than I had last seen. Iqbal applied the gauze and wound the bandage with gentleness and a deftness, which indicated some first aid training, and that he had probably done it many times on the battlefields in the North African Campaign.

It was time to sit down again, the silence of the hot sultry night was broken only by the buzzing of the pestering mosquitoes and the chatter of the small lizards (chit chats) on the walls snapping up the moths and other insects attracted by the hurricane lantern. The occasional crack of rifle fire indicated that the police were trying to enforce a curfew or the soldiers in the signal box were firing indiscriminately to discourage any movement around the station area. I rested for an hour or so unable even to doze. Iqbal lay on the floor, while Bert tossed and turned in his half recumbent position in his chair. The four officials, weary from their long vigil, chatted in subdued tones, sitting at their table just outside the small room. They didn't seem to sleep at all.

It must have been nearing midnight when I decided to visit Hussein. Iqbal followed. In the 22 ton open wagon, the bodies had been laid in two rows, three or four high with a few extra thrown on top. Hussein was just about to come and ask what to do next, when we appeared. We needed to release the brake lever, get the crowbars, and change the points again. The wagon was soon in motion and with little effort. The main track sloped slightly down hill away from the station. Within a couple of minutes, the wagon was gaining momentum and as we stopped applying the crowbars, the creaking, lumbering wagon disappeared into the darkness trailing the coupling across the sleepers, which we could still hear clanking long after we lost sight of the wagon. We changed the points again and levered in the next open wagon from the siding. We left Hussein and his gang to load the remainder of the bodies, he now knew exactly what to do and the down gradient of the track saved a lot of effort.

The night was sultry as we picked our way amongst the figures on the dimly lit platform. Bert was standing at the entrance to the platform from the main hall. A good sign, I thought, if he wanted to exercise, that his wound was on the mend. "There's been more sniping from the signal box," he said, "and one of the officials asked if either of us could drive." "Yes I can drive," I replied, "and we did hear the firing about seven or eight shots while we were moving the wagons." "I'll tell him," he said, and turned away to inform the official.

I was curious and was about to follow, when Iqbal gently took my arm and ushered me a few paces past the entrance. "Lend me your pistol sahib, please, and I will put an end to the firing from the signal box." I was taken aback by his request and hesitated before replying – "Its too risky for you," trying to put him off. "There will be three or four of them there and one will be on guard all the time," I continued trying to dissuade him. "I will have the darkness, the element of surprise and Allah on my side," he replied, with such confidence; while holding my hand between both of his, he raised my hand and touched his forehead, almost begging.

Reluctant as I was, I produced the pistol from my small pack, which I carried about continuously, never leaving it out of my sight. "I have handled many of these in North Africa," he said, removing the magazine from the pistol grip and cocking the pistol. Checking the breach was empty, he gently squeezed the trigger and controlled the return of the breach block to its forward position. He was obviously familiar with this weapon, I thought, as he snapped the fully loaded magazine back into the base of the grip. He tucked the pistol into his shirt and once again took my hand in both of his. "I will be back in an hour," he said, glancing at his watch.

I stood and watched him pick his way towards the southern end of the platform, the way we had come in the night before, in the direction of the signal box. I was excited and apprehensive at the same time; I could feel a cold trickle of perspiration down my back. Either a brave man or a fool, I thought, as he disappeared into the shadows at the end of the platform without once looking back.

I returned to the small room where Bert was huddled in his chair, but wide-awake. I flopped into my chair exhausted, but eager to hear what Bert had to say, as he seemed excited. "A bus is coming tomorrow and they want you to drive it to Pakistan." I could not get all the questions out quick enough but Bert gradually unfolded the details.

It seemed that while I was away with Hussein, another official had appeared with the four officials at the station. He apparently spoke some English and told Bert that if we would drive a bus to Pakistan he would arrange for it to be at the station the following day, and if we could leave after dark, he would give us 'protection' and a guide. "Pakistan is a hell of a long way from here," I said, "did he say anything about fuel, who is going to be on the bus, what about the protection, what form is that going to take?" No he had not mentioned anything but would be back in the morning to give us more information.

As I lay slumped in the chair, smacking at the mosquitoes, my mind was racing backwards and forwards between what Bert had told me, the possibility of getting on our way home, and Iqbal creeping about in the darkness, out by the signal box, I must have dozed off for a while from almost complete exhaustion. I awoke at the sound of a metallic clatter, automatically glanced at my watch; it was just after four in the morning. Iqbal was sitting on the floor examining his booty. "Look, sahib, look," he said, showing me his winnings and proud of his achievements. Two 303 Lee Enfield rifles, two sten guns, and a .38 Webley pistol, with an ample supply of ammunition to fit all three weapons.

"There were five of them, sahib, five," he repeated excitedly, "I killed them all," he said, with no more display of emotion than if he had been talking about rabbits. He returned my pistol and digging into his pocket gave me two generous helpings of 9mm ammunition, some falling to the floor in the semi darkness.

He couldn't contain himself. He explained in great detail, his eyes dilated with excitement, how he had crept up to the signal box, ascended the steps, pistol in hand, and shot the sentry at point blank range. The other four, who were asleep on the floor, hardly had time to gather their senses when he shot them in quick succession, where they lay. He had quickly gathered up the arms, ripped the telephone hand set from the box and thrown it into the yard below. "Fools," he said with contempt in his voice, "not real soldiers, only jats (farmers) in uniform."

There was no more sleep for me that night, while Iqbal and Hussein carefully examined each weapon, clicking the bolts backwards and forwards, fondling the breach blocks of the stens and reassembling them. They oiled the moving parts and used the pull through stored in the base of the rifle butts as though they were preparing for a sergeant major's inspection in the morning.

Bert slept through it all, quite unaware of the events of the night before. Seven o'clock brought more steaming tea, sweet as honey, with freshly baked naan bread still warm from the oven. I related to Bert, the excitement of the previous hours, while the four of us dunked the bread in the tea and ate our morning breakfast.

With little else to do, Bert and I sat around while the two sepoys took the first aid box with half a dozen table cloths from the dining room and attended to the injured on the platform, tearing up the table cloths for bandages and sparingly using the pungent yellow powder from the jar.

There were ghastly wounds to be attended and the women were most reluctant to expose any part of the body above the elbow or knee. Hussein organised another body loading party, shouting instructions with his new found confidence and a sten gun slung over his shoulder. Another party resumed clearing the drains between the tracks using the fire hoses. The women and children squatting or sprawling out on the platforms, gathered in little groups murmuring among themselves, nursing the babies or consoling the toddlers, but seemingly quite resigned to their situation, in their belief that the all merciful Allah would see them through whatever adversity he wished them to suffer.

With another two wagons loaded and levered away from the platform and all the drains having been washed down, the afternoon was upon us.

The scorching August sun pushed the temperature to 110 – 112 degrees, and with the millions of flies continuously pestering, a drowsy hush fell over the station. There had been no shooting from the signal box that morning and four or five women had made successful trips to the hand pump outside the station returning with two buckets of cool water each time, pumped from a well probably some two hundred feet deep and fed by a spring.

Two of the officials were already asleep sitting in their chairs head down on the table. Bert was asleep again, so I flopped down in the wicker chair beside him and was soon overtaken by drowsiness. A lack of sleep the night before, and being weary beyond words, I slept for about four hours.

I awoke to excited chattering and a bit of shouting and hand clapping, to find a three ton Chevy truck, half converted to a bus, had been reversed into the ticket hall through the massive archway, which formed the entrance. "This is the bus you must drive to Pakistan," said one of the excited officials. He answered all my questions as quickly as I put them to him. The roof and sides of the bus were complete; the wooden frame was clad in sheet metal and the chassis extended some six feet to increase the carrying capacity. There were no seats just a bare wood plank floor, no glass in the windows, and a cutaway section in the body where an entry exit door should have been.

Inside the bus the wooden framework was completely exposed and the sheet metal on the inside was unpainted. Two fifty six gallon drums, one on each side, lay in cradles directly above the original fuel tanks of the vehicle. The tank and the drums had been connected, by a rubber hose, with a crude 'on off' tap, fitted to the drum; the whole outfit reeked of petrol, in spite of the open aspect of the body. I tapped the drums, they were full; a wet patch around each screwed bung indicated that they were ill fitting and allowed leakage when the fuel was sloshing about inside. The vehicle was almost new and had most probably been bought at an auction sale of War Department equipment at the end of the war; the front end was still painted in wartime 'olive green drab'.

The engine started instantly and all the ancillary equipment was in working order; there were no doors to the cab, the glass from the cab rear window had been removed, the heavy-duty military tyres had been replaced with normal road tyres and all were in good condition.

"You must leave tonight," the official insisted, and proceeded to give a list of instructions. A guide would be provided and we were to go straight to Ludhiana, to an address in the city, where we were to pick up a very wealthy Muslim family, who were expecting us to take them to Pakistan. The head of the family was apparently in the transport business and the truck (bus) belonged to him and was one of the few vehicles that had survived the burning and looting in Ambala city.

There was little preparation to be made, Bert had nothing to carry and only possessed the clothes he was wearing and I only had my small pack, which now contained very little more than shaving tackle, toothbrush, soap and towel, my documents and pistol.

Iqbal and Hussein both expressed a wish to accompany us and this was agreed by the official in exchange for one rifle and a Sten gun. By this time it was known that Iqbal had wiped out the group in the signal box and he had been on the receiving end of much praise and back slapping. The next few hours were quiet but as soon as it was dark, the lentils and rice appeared again, and though now monotonous, were nevertheless welcome.

It was fourteen hours since we were dunking naan bread in tea for breakfast. At nine that night we were all impatient to get moving but we were held up awaiting the arrival of the guide. We were in the process of handing over the rifle, Sten gun with magazines fully charged, and the spare ammunition, to the official, when shooting started again from the signal box. All eyes turned towards Iqbal, but it was Hussein who insisted that he should go this time, against all advice, for I knew they would be prepared and alert for any repeat of the previous nights intrusion. He was adamant about his task and though his comrade Iqbal tried to dissuade him, it was to no avail. After handshakes all round and much patting on the back, he skipped out into the semi darkness of Platform 1, carrying a Sten gun and two magazines, in the direction of the signal box.

Hussein had not been gone but a few minutes, when the guide appeared, an old man with a grey beard, still showing large patches of henna colouring, proclaiming to all he had performed his religious duty in attending the Haj in Mecca. He carried in one hand, an ancient single barrel shot gun and proudly displayed six shotgun cartridges in a bandolier across his chest. The other hand held a small bundle with the handle of a tiffin carrier protruding from it, presumably his next couple of meals. He was impatient to leave at once, as he had scouts out along the way, who were expecting us. I was reluctant to leave without Hussein but was assured by the official that he would put him on the next bus out a few nights later. Iqbal too, was torn between waiting for his comrade and taking the opportunity to leave. "We go now," I said to the official; Bert and Iqbal climbed into the passenger compartment and the guide and I prepared to ride in the cab. I started the engine. "No lights," said the guide and we moved off driving down a flight of six shallow steps which led up to the ticket hall.

We had barely moved a hundred yards, when the sound of heavy automatic fire reached us, from the direction of the station. The intensity of the fire indicated more than one person firing. Our thoughts immediately went out to Hussein, but no one mentioned it. I felt a twinge of anguish at the loss, for Hussein and Iqbal had surely saved my life in that field of burning tiger grass.

Iqbal immediately requested to stop the truck, as he wanted to return to the station. I tried hard to persuade him to stay with us. But he was determined to return and without explanation dismounted from the truck and disappeared into the darkness in the direction of the station. The guide was giving precise instructions all the time, periodically he waved or called out to an unseen figure crouched behind a wall or thick shrubbery.

There was no movement on the dimly lit roads, the curfew was being enforced and we were being directed around the small groups of police who were patrolling. We travelled very slowly, but within half an hour we were clear of the city limits and out in the rural area, without any encounter. We joined the Grand Trunk Road, at which point, a figure appeared waving a lantern. I stopped and the guide and scout spoke for a few minutes, small bundles of papers were exchanged and a heavy cash box given to the guide. The scout extinguished his lantern and disappeared as quickly as he had appeared.

We drove on and within a few miles, we reached the mighty Sutlej River, one of the five rivers of the Punjab, the road and railway bridges ran parallel, only a couple of hundred yards apart. At this time of the year, August, the river was a mile wide and in full spate, due to the monsoon rain in the Himalayan Mountains. The volume of water was controlled at the Bhakra Dam further up stream, where my father and I had often gone fishing.

In the fast fading light we saw a stationary train silhouetted against the sky, about thirty flat wagons standing on the bridge. There was some activity on several of the wagons. I stopped the truck to take a closer look. The wagons were piled high with what I first thought were sacks. With a closer look, I realised that the sacks were bodies; the activity was the disposal of the bodies by heaving them into the river. I estimated three to four thousand bodies on the train. As soon as I realised what was happening, we made a hasty departure from the scene. The millions of turtles in the river would soon devour the evidence.

Ludhiana was approximately one hundred miles and we made good progress. We saw no signs of the army or police but passed a slow moving convoy of about 20 bullock carts loaded to the sky with household possessions, each one with a hurricane lantern swinging wildly from the end of a pole, and a male member of the family either leading the animals or riding on the cart.

A few words were exchanged between the guide and the convoy. They were refugees – all from one village, which they had left to the last man and were heading for Pakistan. They had no idea how far it was or what the dangers were, they only knew they were heading in the right direction and with Allah's help would get there some time.

How many more refugee trains? Many thousands tried to escape the slaughter resulting in one of the largest population movements in history. Richard Symonds estimates at the lowest, half a million perished and twelve million became homeless. *Illustrated London News/Mary Evans Picture Library*

A boozy Sunday morning after a night on patrol.
William Jewel married Pam Odgers 1946 Hastings
Calcutta.   *Author's own collection.*

Tony Hearne in Eden Gardens Calcutta 1946 –
footloose and fancy free.   *Author's own collection.*

Vehicle recovery team during riots in Calcutta May 1947.   *Author's own collection.*

The migration was a "massive exercise in human misery," wrote Bourke-White. A small convoy of Muslim refuges on the road. They have no idea of the distances involved to Pakistan or how many days they will be on the road: many never reached their destination slaughtered to a man.   *Margaret Bourke White/gettyimages*

Men, women and children who died in the rioting were cremated on a mass scale. Villagers even used oil and kerosene when wood was scarce   *Margaret Bourke-White/gettyimages*

More refugees - travel as far as you can. Railway station in the Punjab.
Illustrated London News/Mary Evans Picture Library

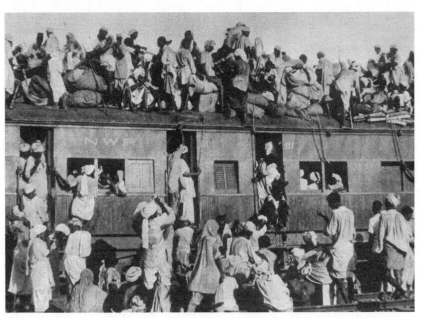

Muslim Refugees heading for Pakistan. Travellers could be days under such conditions. There were many
casualties. *Illustrated London News/Mary Evans Picture Library*

The author's mother- dressed for duty at the British Military Hospital, Lahore Cantonment during World War II.
Author's own collection.

Reference: 23

Magistrate Gerald Frederick Hearne and his wife Nellie Ethel White taking colonial justice to the remotest parts of the empire – the Kulu Valley. The last 40 miles reached on horsebackand no matter how remote he always looked the sahib.

Author's own collection.

The Empire Ken.   *Author's own collection.*

Chapter 8
The Grand Trunk Road

TODAY THE name would imply a super highway – three or four lanes in each direction, I don't know if there have been any improvements, as I have never been back. In 1947 however, The Grand Trunk Road was no more than a two lane, (one in each direction) unlit road that had taken an unmerciful pounding from thousands of military convoys during the war years. There was no planned maintenance of the surface, just patch and mend, as the Public Works Department could not spare the money from their budget. The road started in Calcutta and terminated in Peshawar some 1400 miles away. Two vehicles could barely pass without getting the nearside wheels off the tarmac, into a four-inch layer of dust or slush depending on the season. Every conceivable form of transport used the road; bullock carts, cycles, buses, horse drawn vehicles, military convoys and a few private cars, as it was the only hard surface road between major towns.

The road and railway track crossed many times during the entire length. The crossings were protected by manually operated double gates, which opened outwards across the road. Flooding of the road was a normal occurrence, especially during the monsoon season. These were the normal and expected conditions when we left Ambala for Ludhiana. The guide continued to give instructions, lights off, lights on, turn right, turn left, stop at the next junction; we must wait for the next scout. The journey of one hundred miles had taken ten hours and we entered the city through narrow lanes hardly wide enough to accommodate the width of the vehicle. We left paint on a few walls and collected scratches and dents along the bodywork.

The centre of the city was burning fiercely; we had seen the pall of smoke from many miles away. I was still getting instructions from the guide, when we came to a well-constructed three-storied building, which I was told was the home of the family we had come to collect and take to Pakistan. When I looked up to the third floor balcony, I was horrified to see the entire family, an adult male, two adult women, and five children, ranging in age from about five to twelve, all hanging from the railings. The guide just shook his head and told me to drive to the mosque a couple of hundred yards away in the square, where there was a fountain still dripping water from an ornamental bowl into a much larger bowl on a plinth.

As soon as it became known that we were heading for Pakistan, we were besieged by a crowd of six or seven hundred men, women and children pleading to be taken. Men were offering thousands of rupees and the women offering all their jewellery to secure a place. They started to clamber over the vehicle to get in, when a uniformed Indian Police Officer, a Muslim, climbed on top of the cab, drew his service pistol and threatened to shoot anyone who would not get off the bus. The crowd jeered and booed and hurled abuse at him and his relations. Nevertheless they dismounted from the vehicle and formed a tight circle around the skeleton bus.

I agreed, I had no option, to take only women and children, and after a three-hour delay, we boarded fifty-six women and children all with pathetic little bundles. They sat on the bare boards; many were standing having tied themselves to the framework of the body of the bus. When not another mouse could have been squeezed on, the police officer wished us well. "God be with you on your journey".

Waving his pistol about, he cleared a way through the crowd, which by this time had grown to two thousand. The bus moved off slowly creaking in every joint of the bodywork, the nose high in the air, due to the weight. The crowd was cheering, many were weeping at seeing their relatives leaving and the more defiant ones shouted "Pakistan Zindabad" – "Long live Pakistan."

We rejoined the Grand Trunk Road a couple of miles outside the city, after a difficult exit, having to avoid burning buildings and twice having to reverse out of streets, which were too narrow. I was relieved to see the open road ahead of me, but it did not last for long. There were clouds of smoke ahead and within a few minutes, we drew level with what had been a convoy of refugees, consisting of some 20 or 30 bullock carts; bodies were scattered on both sides of the road, slashed, axed or bludgeoned to death, hundreds, an entire village probably, even the animals had been slaughtered. Young women and girls naked and violated with their throats cut and mutilated; men just butchered. There was not a soul alive; at a rough guess I would say five or six hundred bodies.

I drove down the road and tried to avoid most of the bodies but could not avoid running over some. The passengers in the back were weeping and wailing, screaming, hysterical with shock. The bullock carts were burning. From the blood on the road I could tell it was not more than an hour since the slaughter had taken place, as the blood had not congealed on the tarmac. The old guide sat impassively next to me, clutching his shotgun, and tears streaming down his cheeks, he could not speak, and he could not look at the scene anymore and bent his head forward in complete dejection.

I did not stop to investigate; there was no evidence to suggest the military were involved, as I did not see any bodies with bullet wounds or empty cartridge cases lying about. I wished I had my camera.

With the engine screaming and the temperature gauge getting near the over heating mark, I managed second gear and then third to get away from the carnage.

The open road once again afforded relief, but it was to be short lived. The truck was not easy to control; the overloading in the back had made the front wheels lose some traction and constant corrections were necessary at the steering wheel in order to maintain a straight course. Every nut and bolt was squeaking, hitting a pothole in the road caused such jolting and thumping that I had misgivings that we might break a main spring.

Progress towards our next main town, Julandhar, only eighty or so miles away, was very slow. The undulation in the road necessitated frequent changes in gear to maintain reasonable momentum. A few miles later, coming over the brow of a slight rise in the landscape, a shallow lake of water revealed itself, as far as the eye could see. The road was completely submerged, at first, just a few inches deep. I changed down to first gear; the problem was keeping the vehicle on the invisible tarmac. A jolting on either the left or the right side indicated the wheels were off the road.

A reasonable course was held by watching the telegraph poles on the side of the road, which ran parallel to the tarmac, about thirty feet from the edge. We endured nearly four hours of this walking speed, with few stretches of the road visible above the water due to the undulating land, and accompanied by the whining of the engine in low gear and the intense summer heat which sapped our energy and reduced concentration.

"Where is all this water coming from?" I asked the guide. There had been no rain on the plains for weeks. He shook his head. I learned later that one of the main irrigation canals off the Sutlej River had deliberately had all the sluice gates opened to flood the land and impede the refugee convoys. Who was responsible for this action will probably never be known, but it was indicative of the collaboration between the Government Irrigation Department and the military.

As we progressed very slowly, the water got deeper: from just a few inches it was now fifteen inches deep and showed signs of flowing rather than being still water. Keeping the vehicle on the tarmac became more difficult. Speed was reduced to less than walking pace.

Grotesquely, bloated bodies began to float across the road; others snagged or pressed against an obstacle, by the current, were becoming more frequent. As another short stretch of road became visible above the water, a railway level crossing gate was closed across the road, as though a train was due. On closer examination, I found the gates chained, with a stout padlock; this was another impediment to the refugee convoys. I examined the chain and the lock, the lock bore the unmistakeable markings "WD" and the broad arrow ^ 1941, indicating War Department property. The only conclusion I could arrive at was, that the military had applied the constriction.

There was no way we could cut the chain, and the lock, of good quality, (Made in England), would, without a key, tax the best of locksmiths. We wasted an hour putting the nose of the truck against the metal gates and pushing in first gear, increasing the pressure, until the lock showed signs of distorting. I began to fear we might burn out the clutch; the engine smelled hot, and there was a general smell of burning. Suddenly with a snap the lock burst open and we unchained the gate. We now had to repeat the action on the other side of the railway track, only this time we had to pull instead of push.

Bert, who all these hours had been buried under a mountain of bodies in the back, managed to extricate himself, and got down to see what he could do.

I explained what we had done on the first gate and that I was doubtful if the clutch would stand another hour of punishment. He examined the second gate, with its heavy chain, a twin of the lock on the first gate. He wandered off to the level crossing keepers hut, only a few yards away, there was no one there, but he returned with a couple of five foot long crow bars.

With a lot of swearing, sweating, heaving and pushing we lifted one side of the gate off its hinges, and levered it , still chained to its partner, sufficiently far over to allow the truck to pass through: it had taken less than twenty minutes. Bert smiled at me, put his index finger to his temple as if to say, "You have to have it up here mate!" I was more than pleased at his experience.

The railway track ran on an embankment and was about twelve feet above the level of the water. The motor road dipped down and within a couple of hundred yards we again found the tarmac underwater, and speed was once again reduced to walking pace. Bert was now sitting in front with the guide and myself; there was not much conversation, everyone was completely exhausted, and I would have gladly let him drive for a while, but he could not drive, plus his leg was now so painful and stiff, I doubt if he could have coped with the constant gear changing.

Progress was very slow, the water being about fifteen inches deep, "Left a bit, right a bit". Bert was doing his best to help. Every so often bodies appeared mostly submerged and it was impossible to avoid running over them, sometimes exploding with a sickening plop like a bursting balloon. The light was failing now and within half an hour it would be pitch black; no twilight in the tropics. In the failing light, bullock carts, axle deep in water, abandoned on the side of the road, began to appear; at first, it was just one or two together, then three and four, and then a whole string of carts about perhaps twenty or thirty. Bodies floated everywhere, half submerged; bulls hung slaughtered, still harnessed to the shafts with bloated bodies showing above the water.

Progress was so slow that it was dark before we passed the lead cart of the convoy. In spite of the possibility of being seen from miles away I was compelled to put on the headlamps, we could not stop in the middle of this lake of misery.

A mile or so further on, the tarmac rose out of the water, as the lights picked up the glistening wet surface we noticed some movement about one hundred yards ahead. I approached very slowly till the dipped lights focused on the object of movement about twenty yards ahead.

We alighted to investigate, it was heart breaking. A young woman, or girl, no more than sixteen, naked, was crawling out of the water on all fours.

I moved the truck forward for a closer examination. She had four sword slashes across her back from shoulder to waist, from eight to ten inches long and gaping wide in the heat of the day, possibly twelve hours old. She was unable to speak, though her eyes were open and she was semi-conscious, we lifted her out of the last few feet of water on to the tarmac, where the water had receded. Three men stood totally impotent, without even a first aid kit, there was nothing we could do. We turned her on her side, horror of horrors, her face was swollen to the size of a football, her nose and lips had been cut off, her ears had been cut off, and the nipples of her breasts had been removed. Her eyes were just slits in the swollen face, she did not blink, she was in a deep state of shock. It was a miracle that she was still alive and that she still had that all-powerful human instinct of self-preservation and strength to crawl out of the water. I could not stand it anymore, and although no word was spoken before or after the event, I drew my pistol and shot her twice in the head.

God alone knows what indignities and humiliation that unfortunate child had inflicted upon her before being left half dead. She must have resisted tooth and nail, to have warranted such utter brutality meted out to her.

I am sure, if she could have spoken she would only have said, "Thank you". After all these years I can still clearly visualise the horror, as if it occurred only yesterday. We could not possibly have left her there alive to be torn apart piecemeal by vultures and carrion crows by day or jackals by night.

I needed that reasoning psychologically, for the justification of my own seemingly inhuman behaviour or I would have suffered from a guilt complex for the remainder of my life. I trust others will judge me mercifully and have empathy with my logic.

We got back into the truck without a word spoken.

The road was now above the water and the water level seemed to be receding, but I had to drive very cautiously as sections of the road had been washed away, leaving only the hard core under layers.

"Sahib," the guide broke the silence, "we are coming to Julandhar soon". The glow in the sky told me we were eight to ten miles from the city. We progressed cautiously watching for lights, which would indicate either police or military patrols. We entered the city from the east. The streets were deserted; it seemed like a dead city. We parked under a dim, flickering street lamp in the yard of the railway station, only a few yards from the main entrance. I walked the few yards to platform one, not a soul in sight. I looked up and down the line, nothing moved. The huge platform clock showed exactly nine o'clock and I saw the minute hand move. A distant signal showed red.

I retraced my steps towards the truck when I noticed a flickering light from an open fire. I walked over, gripping my pistol behind my back. To my surprise I found a Hindu vendor sitting cross legged on a mat, with a zinc bath mounted on bricks, with the smouldering and flickering flames of a cow dung pat fire under the bath tub, full to the brim with a pale liquid, with a whisper of steam rising off the surface.

At that moment I was joined by the guide. They spoke. "How much is the tea?" "One rupee a cup," came the reply, normally one pice – at sixty-four to the rupee. Before I could raise a finger, the guide pointed his shotgun and shot the vendor at point blank range. "Cheating bastard," was his only comment. "Bring the truck closer Sahib, we will give the people a drink." We found a stack of earthenware cups close at hand and the guide set about distributing the tea to the women and children.

It was the only liquid they had had since leaving Ludhiana, about 26 hours earlier. I was apprehensive that the sound of the shot would bring the police or military down on us, so I moved the truck on to a small grassy area behind an oleander hedge. We were all exhausted, the guide continued to distribute the tea, some dismounted to stretch their legs. We found seven women and three children dead in the truck; they had died of dehydration and heat stroke. We unloaded the bodies and left them on the grassy patch in front of the station.

I lay down on the grass, which felt cool after the heat of the day, using the seat cushion from the driver's seat as a pillow I fell into a sleep of oblivion.

I was woken by Bert at the first break of dawn. "We better make a move it's getting light." I had slept, virtually unconscious, for five hours. Within minutes we were moving again, leaving behind the ten dead bodies plus the vendor hidden behind the hedge.

Amritsar was the next major town. Under instructions from the guide we rejoined the Grand Trunk Road. Navigating fifty miles of clear roads, we only passed only one small convoy of refugees. We did not enter Amritsar town, a Sikh stronghold, it would have been suicide. We were now on the last leg of the journey. Lahore, our intended destination was only forty miles away.

About sixteen miles beyond Amritsar, there was a military roadblock manned by a small contingent from a Rajput Regiment. We were flagged down at the zig-zag barrier made from tar barrels filled with stones. It was impossible to crash through and it would have been an invitation to death as they were all armed with sand-bagged defensive positions on either side of the road with LMGs (light machine guns – Bren guns) clearly displayed.

We were approached by a VCO (Viceroy Commissioned Officer). He spoke English "You cannot go, you are all prisoners of war." I tried to reason with the man explaining that we only had women and children on board, and that if he made us prisoners he would have to feed us and give us medical attention. A British major who commanded the detachment on border duty, supported my argument, though without much firmness. His own position was precarious to say the least. After some argument, some soldiers climbed aboard to search the truck for arms, at the same time relieving the women of any jewellery that was visible and demanding to search their ragged little bundles of worldly possessions. Bert had his revolver confiscated; the one he had taken from the VCO on the train, and received a stunning slap from the VCO. I had difficulty in restraining him from attacking the VCO. The guide had already been disarmed of his shotgun and received punches and kicks and a bone crushing thump on the back with the butt of a rifle.

"You can go," said the VCO. "But this fellow cannot go." At the same time pointing to the guide prostrate on the ground, having been felled with the blow from the rifle butt. "Go Sahib, go quickly," at the same time stretching from his prone position to touch my shoes. "Allah will bless you." We wasted no time in getting back into the truck. The British Major, who had played a minimal role in the negotiations came to the entrance of his tent, and gave the thumbs up sign. I never got his name.

Chapter 9
The Border Post

WE MOVED off through the Indian roadblock. We had barely covered twenty yards when there was a burst of fire from a sten gun. Bert instinctively looked back and saw the guide motionless on the ground, being repeatedly kicked by a couple of sepoys.

The road was clear ahead, we gradually picked up speed and I felt easier that we were now only about thirty miles from Lahore. We had only covered about two miles when I heard rifle fire. We were being followed by a Jeep and two sepoys standing in the back, were deliberately shooting into the back of the truck. I could hear the bullets ripping into the bodywork. "Step on it for God's sake," said Bert. I did not need his encouragement; my foot was already flat to the floorboards. There was little response from the overloaded vehicle. The Jeep followed for a mile pumping a steady flow of rifle fire into the back of the truck, but then started to drop back.

Suddenly the windscreen of our vehicle disintegrated into a shower of glass splinters accompanied by the sound of bullets striking the back of the cab. "Get down, get down," shouted Bert, and I did. I was sitting on the floor of the cab; my left foot on the accelerator, my right foot on the running board, there were no doors to the converted truck, peering round the body work to see where I was going. One hundred yards ahead was a Pakistani army border post. They had heard the shooting and thought the Indian Army was attacking their border post, and they were defending themselves. In my crouched position I fumbled for the headlight switch and flicked them on and off repeatedly in a feeble attempt to convey we were 'friendly'.

The shooting from behind stopped; a few more shots from the front and then silence. I stopped the truck twenty feet from the barrier and alighted, arms raised high in the air, to face twenty men, rifles, stens and LMGs pointed menacingly at me. I just half turned and pointed at the jeep some one hundred yards away which was in the process of turning round to return to its own territory. "Indian Army," I shouted.

The response was instantaneous. "Maro sala," somebody shouted. It seemed that every weapon at the post was being fired, including the LMGs. The jeep did not complete the manoeuvre and burst into flames. One man jumped off the jeep, his uniform burning. I could not look back. He had been completely soaked in fuel from the exploding petrol tank; he struggled frantically to free himself from the burning material of his uniform, screaming in agony, dancing like a live puppet, all in vain. He was incinerated where he stood and his prostrate figure continued to burn long after he was dead.

After a very hurried and trembling explanation of the situation, I was allowed to move the truck beyond the barrier and presumably into Pakistan territory. I did not feel much safer and Bert was even more agitated, as he could not understand any of the conversation. "What's happening?" "Can we leave?" "How far to Lahore?" The questions came thick and fast.

In moving the truck behind the barrier, there was a trail of blood, which had dripped through the floorboards of the truck. We immediately realised that many of those unfortunates who were huddled in the rear, had been hit by the shooting from the jeep. A working party was hurriedly mustered with the Havaldhas barking orders, with much waving of arms and wringing of hands. The unloading of the passengers began.

There were many survivors, but those at the rear had taken the brunt of the shooting, receiving multiple bullet wounds, as they had formed a barrier protecting those who were in the forward section of the vehicle. About twenty bodies were put to one side, all women and children. The wounded were segregated in another group, some with two or three body wounds, soon to die. There was no doctor at the border post. The first aid box was exactly that, a paltry collection of a few bandages, half a dozen battlefield dressings, the inevitable bottle of sulphonamide and iodoform powder and rusty scissors.

Even if there had been a doctor, with a more comprehensive set of equipment, it would have been impossible to attend to the women with body wounds, as this would have necessitated the removal of clothing, quite out of the question in a Muslim society. They were put in a group and quite literally allowed to bleed to death. Those with superficial wounds got some attention but even so the women were vehemently reluctant to expose any part of their anatomy above the knee or elbow.

Those that were unscathed sat in a passive group in total shock, unable to speak and staring blankly with wide eyes; some were still wearing the "burkha", the all enveloping tent like gown which covers the body from head to foot, with a mesh like window for the eyes.

They were in a trance, shocked and unknowing of their situation, uncaring what happened to them. Children were totally exhausted either crying for want of nourishment or dehydration, others asleep or lifeless, still being clutched to the bosom by young mothers completely oblivious of their surroundings, resigned.

The British Major in command of the outpost was of little help, he was himself, in a semi state of shock, unable to grasp the enormity of the tragedy unfolding right there in front of him. He was a youngish man who may well still be alive today, but in his late eighties or early nineties. He will have never lost the images at that border post, and probably suffered bouts of depression for the rest of his life.

The border post consisted of about 25 or 30 ridge tents neatly set in rows. In military jargon they were known as 180 pounders the weight being determined by their fully packed condition including supporting poles ready for erection. Along side there were three large marquee tents; one used as a store house for rations and the other as a cookhouse. The third marquee was the domain of the quartermaster.

Considering the very short organisational period after independence, the camp was well laid out. The third marquee tent was for the sole use of the quartermaster who ate, slept and performed all his other official functions within sight of his abode. It contained the ammunition for the whole company, no shortages there, spare clothing, his office and all the store accounting ledgers and files which substantiated his vital role in the company. This paraphernalia seemed to give him the 'God given' authority to strut about the camp with the air of the Angel Gabriel. With his row of medal ribbons, huge greying walrus moustache, broad shoulders and a slight stoop betraying his years of service and age, he was still a formidable figure of a man, not to be argued with by anyone below the rank of British Major.

The camp was set up in a flat dusty plain, among a sparse spread of babool trees also known as camel thorn trees recognised by their little leathery foliage and two inch long vicious thorns which could penetrate normal clothing or even leather gloves.

Near the cookhouse was parked a two thousand gallon water bowser, with an armed guard and by the quartermaster's domain, a neatly stacked supply of 5 gallon jerry cans of petrol and diesel. This supply was surrounded by a six foot high barbed wire fence gated and locked. Every drop had to be signed for and entered into his ledgers.

We had been persuaded to stay a day at the border post. We were assured that the Muslim League and Red Crescent would be coming, as a small party had been sent to Lahore, less than 20 miles away, to explain the situation and bring some relief. There was no telephone at the post. It was no surprise that the one day stay was prolonged to two days.

During this stay, Bert and I made a joint statement taken down by a Subedhah Major (V.C.O.) in Urdu. There were many questions and he became more alarmed as the events unfolded. Bert was reluctant to talk too much, as it seemed he did not want to reveal any details of his identify. I suspected he was a deserter from his regiment but he never admitted it to me. He studiously avoided the Major, answering his questions with the briefest of explanations. I do not think the major was too concerned about one love sick soldier who had embarked on a 1000 mile hazardous journey to be with the cause of his malady.

The first day at the camp was taken up with burial parties interring the bodies of the dead; the shallow graves were dug by hand into hard dusty soil with 'shovels general purpose'. It seemed half the soldiers at the post were employed on grave digging duties, with bodies conveyed to the grave one at a time on the one 'stretchers canvas' which came from the QM's store.

The second day dawned. Bert and I had slept in a 180 pounder on 'charpoys' next door to the QM's tent. Much of the day was occupied by more grave digging, as some of the wounded had succumbed during the night. One young mother became hysterical when her dead toddler was taken away. The survivors were dwindling in number, twenty had been removed dead from the truck on arrival, six or eight had died the first night, and more would die this second day. The only attention the severely wounded received was occasional sips of water to avoid dehydration, a futile attempt to keep them alive till help arrived. Those who were not wounded sat or lay in whatever little patch of shade they could find, to avoid the scorching heat. Food was supplied from the soldier's cookhouse in mess tins, and though only a pretty monotonous diet of 'dhal and charwal' – lentils and rice, twice a day, with a liberal serving of 'charay' – tea, it was most welcome. Grave digging went on till late evening, as it is customary for the dead to be buried within twenty four hours. More would surely die this second night. There was no sign of the Red Crescent.

Bert and I decided, that come what may we would leave for Lahore the following day. The truck was barely road worthy and, by this time, very low on fuel with no windscreen or lights, and even more bullet holes in the front bodywork. The fuel shortage could only be overcome with the consent of the QM and the Post Commander. A quick swill down with a mug and bucket of water, under a babool tree, before the sun went down, went a long way to alleviating the discomfort of the heat. We were sitting on camping stools outside our tent, applying a liberal application of citronella oil to the exposed areas of skin, to ward off the unwelcome attention of mosquitoes and gnats, when we were summoned to the commanders tent. We each lit hurricane lamps and picked our way gingerly up, over and around the guy ropes of the tents. We were welcomed with more tea, actually poured from a teapot, Officer's Mess type and served with Carnation tinned milk. Another seemingly hundred questions were asked in order that he could complete his log for the day.

It had been a busy day: earlier in the evening we had witnessed the 'mounting of the guard' for the night security of the camp and the manning of sand bagged gun emplacements guarding the fuel dump, ration tent, water bowser. A prowler element of the guard had been organised to keep the jackals away from the recently buried bodies. Jackals are quite accustomed to burrowing, spending much time underground during the day and foraging for rodents and rabbit by night. A pack would have no difficulty in digging down four feet to unearth a body.

The Major was quite distressed about our account of the last few days, the evidence of which was spread around his compound and the shooting up of the jeep. The latter event could easily have set off a major, country wide confrontation.

The Hindu, Sikh and Muslim regiments were spread all over the country and many were on the wrong side of the border. There had not been enough time since the declaration to shuffle all the regiments around and withdraw them to their own territory.

After a short formal discussion, the Major gave each of us a packet of cigarettes, Players Navy Cut, from his well stocked travelling chest; his Regimental Officer's mess no doubt took care of all his needs. The cigarettes were most welcome as I had spent part of the day scrounging 'beries', a crude tobacco leaf cigarette, from anyone who was prepared to part with them.

We picked up our hurricane lanterns to return to our tent, it was now quite dark; we were challenged by the roaming guard. "Who goes there?" blurted out in parrot fashion was followed by a challenge in Urdu. "Friend," I shouted at a couple of unseen figures, lurking in the darkness. "Whose friend?" came the unexpected reply, accompanied by the sound of a bolt ramming home a round into the breach of the MKIV Lee Enfield. We both froze, flummoxed as to what to reply: whose friend was I? I took a few seconds to collect my wits, as a figure appeared dimly lit by the hurricane lamp, rifle at the ready, bayonet fixed and probably a very itchy finger on the trigger. The only reply I could think of, in a flash of a second was "King George's friend" and with great relief came the reply, "Pass friend".

I'm not sure if he knew who King George was or even understood what I had said, but I was sure glad I had listed the King of England as my friend, although it is doubtful if it was reciprocated.

We retreated to our tent, without tripping over any guy ropes. Sitting on our charpoys, we were putting a match to the mosquito coils when a great hullabaloo started at the guard post.

A long line of lights had been seen approaching the camp from the Pakistan side of the border. As this winding snake of lights approached our camp, it was established that it was a convoy of bullock carts, tongas, tumtums and improvised hand carts of refugees of Hindus and Sikhs, fleeing from Pakistan to the other side. Hindus and Sikhs, who normally tolerated each other from a distance, now joined forces to move together under cover of darkness gaining safety in numbers. The convoy was stopped one hundred yards from the camp. By this time the alarm had been sounded and every soldier on the camp was out, in every state of undress, but rifle at the ready. Two bren gun carriers, (tracked vehicles), were stationed at strategic points, spot lights blazing and trained on the head of the convoy. A small party was sent to talk to the leaders; they returned to the camp and, after a pow-wow with the Major, it was decided to let them pass unmolested. They were directed around the camp out into the fields and then back onto the main road avoiding the zigzag barriers which the heavily loaded bullock carts would not have been able to negotiate.

I can only estimate the numbers involved, probably three to four thousand souls perched precariously on the carts. The men walked and hurricane lanterns, suspended beneath each cart swung wildly from side to side, as they rocked and jolted through the fields. There was hardly a sound except for the dry squeak of the wooden wheels, crying out for a bit of lubrication. It took about four hours for the convoy to pass. I did not hear a shot fired, nor did I see anyone molested, although every soldier was on high alert. The slightest provocation would have resulted in a slaughter such as I had witnessed on the journey to the camp. Much of the calm was due to the VCO'S and the Major who insisted that they be allowed to pass peaceably. The peaceful passage was a great credit to the discipline of the army whose obedience and loyalty were indisputable.

It was way past 3 a.m. before the last swinging lamps disappeared from view into the darkness. The camp was 'stood down'. All those who were not on duty retreated to their beds to snatch a few hours sleep before the break of dawn.

There was no clear cut definitive line as to where the border lay. A half mile or mile either way would not have made much difference on that hot dusty plain. I discovered that the post had been situated very close to the village of Waga, about twelve to sixteen miles from the city. I remembered Waga as a collection of mud huts, a mosque, a well with a Persian wheel and stockades for the cattle. As a young boy, about ten years old, I had accompanied my dad and eldest brother to the jheel – overflow lake – on fishing trips.

At that time, about 1935, my father was Lahore Cantonment Magistrate and we lived in an enormous compound with a house designated for the use of the Magistrate, and an imposing Officer's Mess. Victoria Barracks was well within earshot of morning 'reveille' and 'lights out', sounded as regular as clock work, by the duty 'corporal of the bugle' for that day. I was a frequent visitor to the barracks, and although only a small boy, was allowed to exercise the huge horses accompanied by the stable staff. The horses, magnificent animals, were used to haul the artillery pieces and ammunition carriages. I learned to ride these gigantic gentle animals and was tolerated as a 'b' nuisance, by the 'corporal of the horse'. I was eventually recognised as the 'chico' of the Cantonment magistrate, having previously been hauled before the adjutant of the regiment for trespassing on military property.

The fields around Waga were lush with sugar cane, maize, cauliflowers and cabbages; it was run on co-operative lines and was quite prosperous by the standards of the times. I believe the new border post is situated on the same site as the original, or very near to it, with an elaborate gateway straddling the Grand Trunk Road. Two or three times a day the changing of the guard ceremony is carried out, with the hauling up and down of national flags. As the Indian Union has also established a post adjacent to the Pakistani post, the changing of the guard on both sides is carried out with much bugle blowing and drum beating, each side trying to outweigh the other with their immaculate uniforms and exaggerated parade ground movements and rifle drill.

Even now today there are always a small group of village folk on both sides of the border to witness this pantomime of almost puppet like figures performing their rituals. Only the older members of the village remember the carnage that led to the establishment of this joint border post. The remainder stand in wonder and awe at the colourful military antics of their respective armies.

There have been two or three occasions, since 1947, when tensions between the two countries have resulted in sabre rattling and open warfare resulting in Bangladesh breaking away from Pakistan and becoming an independent country. Even today open hostilities exist in the more remote border areas of Kashmir.

The third day dawned: Bert and I awoke, bleary eyed and determined to leave that day. The Major had consented to giving us enough fuel to get to Lahore, on the condition that we took our cargo of 'walking wounded' with us. We had lost more than half of the original passenger load; ten still lay mortally wounded, not in a fit state to travel; about twenty were sufficiently able bodied to withstand the last 12-15 miles.

At about 10 o'clock, having breakfasted on tea and naan bread (no corn-flakes there), we loaded the remaining fit passengers, refuelled the much battered truck and were saying our farewells, when the representatives of the Muslim League rolled into camp in a bus, about ten or twelve in all.

A doctor, a couple of soldiers (the original messengers), half a dozen officials, and a reporter from the Civil and Military Gazette wanted to see and document the events. We were in no mood for further delay and after a short parlay explaining we had already given a full account of the events, we were ready to move.

The Gazette reporter joined Bert and I in the cab; he was to show us the way to Lahore station. We pulled out of Waga outpost about 10.30 a.m., the sun already blistering hot, with all the blessings that Allah could bestow on us and half the complement of the camp, waving us off in silence.

We almost immediately passed Waga village, which was about a quarter mile off the main road, now expanded into a sizeable village with more substantial houses and far more prosperous looking than I remember from 1935.

They even had a bus station, I was told, and had not suffered any disturbances during the intervening years from the termination of the Far East War, August 1945 to the Declaration of Independence in August 1947.

Chapter 10
Homeward Bound

I T WAS WITH considerable relief that we left the border post to cover the last few miles to Lahore Railway Station which had been established as the H.Q of the Muslim League. The reporter with his 'sing song', but grammatically flawless accent, sat on the floor of the cab, one foot on the running board and complete with mill board and clip, scribbled away in short hand. His questions came in rapid fire succession; he was excited at the prospect of getting the first eye witness report from the other side of the border, and would no doubt, be hoping to impress his editor with his scoop.

We soon approached the Sudhar Bazaar area of Lahore Cantonment: we had already passed the locally famous Shalimar Gardens, a green oasis of a park, a legacy of the Moghul rulers of the Punjab, and a memorial to a beautiful wife.

It brought back a flood of memories of those carefree days of the thirties. I clearly remember the brilliant moonlight picnics during the mid-summer months, watching the swimmers in the cool water of the lily pool and the bare footed dancers on the manicured grass enjoying the strains of scratchy gramophone music. I was too young to participate in those colonial high jinx, but can well imagine the sound of the gentle flowing water coupled with the swish of the fountains and the stolen hugs and kisses behind the lush, crimson flowered hibiscus hedges and mauve blankets of the bougainvillea. The whole atmosphere would have been flooded with the heavy fragrance of the night scented jasmine and romantic sparkle of a thousand fire flies.

These wonderful memories were rudely interrupted by the reality of the bazaar created by the honking, tooting and bell ringing of the crowded highway and the raucous vendors haggling over the price of a purchase. Cows and goats wandered unfettered between the market stalls grazing on the discarded greenery from the vegetable carts. Little boys and girls ran alongside the truck, which had been slowed to walking pace, asking for 'baksheesh': the reporter shooed them away with unprintable abuse.

Progress was slow until we cleared the main bazaar area by which time we only had a few more miles to Lahore Station. The forecourt of the station was crowded with tongas, carts and cycle rickshaws, railway coolies, (porters) loading and unloading luggage and bundles of possessions. A train had recently arrived from somewhere further north with refugees hoping to get to India, mostly Hindus and Sikhs, fearful for their lives as they were now in hostile territory.

The newspaper reporter directed us to a marquee in a corner of the station compound. He had valiantly endured the uncomfortable ride since leaving the border post without any complaint. He had pages of shorthand notes which would no doubt impress his superiors at the C & M (Civil & Military Gazette), where Rudyard Kipling had been the editor in earlier times. Inching our way forward through the milling throng, we finally came to a halt beside the tent which was besieged by refugees who had safely managed to cross the border from India. The reporter found an official who seemed to have some authority and pushing and shoving, he brought him to the truck. Talking excitedly, almost shouting at each other to overcome the weeping and wailing of the crowd, he managed to get the basic facts explained, at the same time pointing out the remaining pathetic group huddled in the back of the bus.

Bert and I were too tired to get involved in any further explanations and pushing our way through the crowds , we came to a clearing where he declared his determination to get to Rawalpindi. I offered to take him home for a meal and clean up but he declined. We shook hands and the last I saw of him was a limping figure disappearing into the main entrance of the station.

I did not return to the bullet riddled, blood soaked vehicle but hailed a tonga wallah to take me home. I gave him directions: straight down Mayo Road. There was an unbroken convoy of bullock carts and pedestrians going in the opposite direction; all Muslim refugee families who had crossed the border somewhere between Lahore and Ferozepore. Twenty minutes later, we pulled up outside the gate of number 123 Mayo Road. I paid off the driver. I was home.

There, standing by the side of the dusty road, was my mother, shaded under a huge sheshum tree and beside her, the faithful old khansama – cook – of twenty five years service to the family. She was hot and grimy, with dust laden sweat trickling down from her temples and dripping from her chin. Her straw hat afforded little protection against the dust or heat well over 100 degrees in that August sun. She wiped her face with a wet towel.

The cook was filling the syringes with anti-cholera and typhoid vaccine, while my mother injected the contents into the refugees as fast as she could. The medical equipment had been supplied by the B.M.H. where my mother had worked as a voluntary nurse during the war. There was no time to observe the niceties, no changing needles: arm up, needle in, swiftly followed by another half a dozen arms being presented for the next jab. She could not tell which arm belonged to which body, unless it was a baby; she studiously ignored the continuous pleading of 'Memsahib Memsahib', trying to attract her attention.

The line was a hundred yards long with men, women, children and carts all proceeding at a slow walk. There was a water pipe for watering the garden, just inside the gate. There was a pushing, shoving group struggling to fill whatever container they had, while the mali – gardener – tried to maintain some calm.

"Hello son," and a quick peck on the cheek was all she could manage while another brown arm was thrust forward. There was obviously a great fear that a cholera or typhoid epidemic could break out which would have added to an already catastrophic situation.

Just then a jeep pulled up in a cloud of dust. Out jumped a uniformed figure carrying a cardboard box, Captain Emile, a doctor and old family friend, was delivering a fresh supply of vaccine and needles and at the same time as saying farewell as he and his family were leaving for Australia pronto. The exodus was gaining momentum; there were tearful farewells with the advice to get out while the going was good. I went into the house, a relief nurse was expected within an hour or so and my mother had already been standing at the roadside for four hours.

What luxury, a bath and some clean clothes, raided from my father's wardrobe, we were roughly the same height and size. Mother came in exhausted, Mrs James having taken over. We were able to welcome each other tearfully after several months of separation. Future plans were discussed.

My father, very distressed at my mother's return from England, insisted she return to the UK as soon as possible. He had arranged a berth on a military train to Karachi where she was to take ship on the P&O liner "Maloja". She had the minimum of luggage as all the other heavy packages had already been shipped by Grindlay's Bank who handled most movements between the colony and UK. It was a short reunion as she was leaving in three days. I spent the next few days building a small wardrobe of summer wear, the dursi –tailor – sitting cross legged on the verandah with his ancient Singer running up shirts and trousers. Mother departed for Karachi on schedule amid more tears, for the anticipated long separation.

While waiting to hear about the move to Kuwait, my father pulled a few strings and I was appointed to the position of temporary clerk in the Punjab Civil Secretariat. I hated the job and within a short period had fallen foul of the Head of Department and quit the post, much to the displeasure of my father. I had been forbidden to bring my noisy motorcycle into the secretariat compound where the business of government was still being conducted, after a fashion, with a much depleted staff, the Hindus and Sikhs having abandoned their posts.

The situation in the north Punjab continued to deteriorate very rapidly; the flow of refugees escalated from thousands to hundreds of thousands. The numerous reports of the feuding elements on both sides of the border raised the possibility of a much greater conflict involving the military rather than the civil population. Lahore was very close to the border and my father deemed it injudicious for either of us to stay in the house.

The next nearest town of any size was Rawalpindi. The house was locked up, the car loaded with everything we considered necessary for survival for a few days. The cook and mali were left in charge and we departed for Pindi. The journey was slow but uneventful except for several convoys of refugees heading south. We spent one night at the government rest house (Dak Bungalow) in Jhelum, where we had stayed many times before on fishing trips to the major river of the same name. We had also previously crossed the Chenab River with its intricate network of irrigation canals and dams to store water for the dry season, all maintained and managed by the Irrigation Department.

We reached Pindi the next afternoon having crossed the Soan River, with Topee Park on the right, and the smoking flare stacks of the Attock Oil Company on the left. We spent the night in the modest Savoy Hotel, on

Edwards Road, run by Mr and Mrs Rogers and their son Terry, who were also preparing to join the exodus, if they could find someone to buy the business. Terry was a school contemporary of mine with whom I had lost contact for a few years, we had much to chat about. We spent two days at the hotel and during our hunt for black market petrol and a few more tinned rations, we met Trevor of the North Western Railway Police.

We learned from the hotel servants and others that the bazaar area was in turmoil: Hindu shops were being looted and set alight, beatings and murders were commonplace and armed gangs wandered around, threatening shop keepers for money, snatching jewellery from women and shooting pariah dogs for target practice. The local population was being terrorised, non Muslims being sought out for the purpose of revenge killings. The non-Muslim women were easily identifiable by their dress or caste mark on the forehead, the men, where doubt existed, were expected to quote from the Koran or to expose their genitals to prove they had been circumcised. Failure to convince the inquisitors resulted in severe beatings, resistance meant instant execution on the spot and scores were killed daily. Some Hindu and Sikh men, so frightened for their lives, tried to disguise themselves as Muslim women by donning the 'burka'. Detection resulted in instant execution.

My father had decided that we should take to the hills away from Pindi where there would be less danger. The Anglo-Indian population in the railway colony of Westridge, a few miles distant, had virtually voluntarily restricted themselves to their homes. The military were confined to barracks or quarters in the Cantonment of Chaklala or Victoria Barracks. Old man Rogers was locking up the hotel and dismissing most of the servants. I found him that last evening assembling his shotgun, having ram-rodded and oiled the mechanism. "I'll make sure I take a couple of dozen with me," he said meaning he was prepared to blast anyone who might attack; Mrs Rogers was chain smoking and gripping her tumbler of scotch in trembling hands. I'm quite sure the same precautions were being taken all over the town.

Dad and I spent that night in one room, shotgun and pistol close at hand. We were up early and ready to move when a tonga pulled up with Trevor clutching a bundle of bedding and a small bag. "Can I come with you?" We had already told him of our plans the previous day.

The trains were not running so they did not need railway police for a few days. It was a very tight squeeze as it was a small car, a Ford Anglia, and very heavily loaded. My father took the wheel and we set off for Murree about thirty nine miles away and pretty well up hill all the way. Murree, at an altitude of about four and a half thousand feet in the lower reaches of the Himalayas, was a hill station for the military in summer, and also the location of a girl's boarding convent and Lawrence College, for boys, at Ghohra Guli. It was a tortuous road with many hair pin bends and sheer drops round every corner; the car engine, screamed in second and third gear.

We only saw a couple of buses, going in the opposite direction, fully loaded with passengers inside and with half a dozen more sitting precariously on the roof. No doubt these were the remnants of the Hindu and Sikh population making a last minute hasty get away, having abandoned everything, but not knowing what fate awaited them in Pindi. We eventually got to the post office and bus station in Murree; the town was deserted, shops were shuttered, locked and bolted, except for a few children playing in the street who soon disappeared indoors on seeing us, but continued to peep out through barred windows.

Trevor, being in uniform and with a pistol, seemed to inspire some confidence and a couple of men came out to give us an account of the last few days. There had been severe beatings and a dozen murders of the minority groups; the bodies had been disposed of down the steep hillsides. There was no sign of police or army to prevent these events. After a while, we were offered tea which we gratefully accepted, as we were in no mood to unload all the caboodle in the car to make our own. We took advantage of the break to check the oil and water in the car and without divulging the conditions that existed in Pindi, we were ready to move within the hour.

We took the only road going north to Kashmir, heading for a rudimentary weekend hut which my father had built with redundant railway sleepers while he was district magistrate in Pindi. The hut was big enough to afford shelter for six or eight people and was used as an overnight camp for weekend shooting parties hunting the elusive Orial, a wild mountain goat. In better times, the servants slept in tents around the hut and took care of the catering.

The road to Kashmir immediately descended into the Jehlum Valley; the Jehlum River rises in Kashmir, fed by the melting snows and monsoon rains. At an altitude of four and a half thousand feet, we passed a large military barracks which was used to give the British regiments respite from the searing heat of the plains. It obviously had a strategic value as it was close to the Kashmir border and dominated the main road to Srinagar and the Gilgit pass, a possible entry point to India for a potential enemy, situated in a rugged valley high up in the Karakoram range. The road shadows the valley of the Indus River, for part of the way, to the Chinese border with towering peaks reaching eight thousand metres on both sides. The Nanga Parbat and K2 are the giants in the area.

Kashmir was an independent Indian State with a Hindu ruler but a majority Muslim population. The state was eventually ceded to the Indian Union despite the objections of the majority population, and remains a subject of dispute between Pakistan and India, to this day.

The road continued to descend right down to river level at the crossing point of Kohala, a toll station, just a collection of tiny huts on the Kashmir side of the border a few miles from the river crossing. We paid the toll, and assured the custodians that no beef products were being imported, a strictly prohibited commodity, though this was not strictly true as we had tins of bully beef among our supplies. The presence of Trevor, in uniform, gave us unimpeded passage. We were now in Kashmir with the River Jehlum roaring down the valley, swollen with monsoon rain from a multiple of minor tributaries.

A few miles after crossing the bridge at Kohala, we took a sharp right turn up a steep loose surface mountain track, while the main road continued on in the valley, hugging the river, to the first main town of Baramullah and Srinagar, a further thirty odd miles. Baramullah was the location of St Joseph's College, run by the Mill Hill priests, where I spent one year in 1942. There was also a missionary hospital run by nuns, with a resident lady doctor, Dr. Hardt; it was also the temporary home to a Captain O'Kelly, his wife and two daughters, who attended the convent in Srinagar.

I suspected he was a front line British Intelligence Officer who played a major role in the arrest of Dr Hardt, who it was later revealed was a German and in possession of sophisticated radio equipment capable of reporting weather conditions and troop movements.

The track we took after crossing the river climbed steeply for six hundred yards and was now about three hundred feet above the river, flowing very fast and wild. The track gradually deteriorated till we reached our make shift shelter, at which point it turned into a bridle path undulating and finally descending to river level, about half a mile further on. We now busied ourselves unloading the car, making tea and preparing something to eat as it was now about seven hours since we had left Pindi and we had had nothing to eat since we left the hospitality of the Savoy Hotel. As darkness descended, we made a small fire, cleaned out the rubbish from the hut, and were preparing to turn in for the night.

We drew straws for the first watch; it fell to Trevor who scouted down the bridle path for a couple of hundred yards and returned to take up his position sitting on a box of rations outside the hut. My father and I lay down on the bare bunks covered with blankets against the chilly night. Dad soon fell asleep as he was tired after the drive from Pindi, it was not a long drive but involved much struggling with the steering wheel and frequent gear changes on the mountain roads.

Suddenly, we were hastily and roughly woken by Trevor, and according to earlier planning, grabbed our weapons and scattered into the shrubbery about forty yards from the hut. Trevor had heard voices and the clip clop of horses hooves on the stones of the bridle track and decided it was safer to hide until we established the intentions of the approaching party. We did not have long to wait.

The quiet of the night was shattered by a fusillade of gunfire, both rifle and shotgun, directed at the hut and the surrounding area; it continued for what seemed an interminable period but in fact only lasted two or three minutes. The sound of the shooting echoed and re-echoed between the valley walls and sounded like a hectic firework display on Chinese New Year's Night. It was deafening. Then the shooting stopped, the last echoes died away and the silence of the night was restored except for the rushing torrent in the valley below.

I had lost my father and Trevor in the darkness and lay prone among the thick bushes not daring to call out. I could see the hut by the still flickering flames of the fire where five or six men stood or sat, still firing the odd volley at the illusion of movement caused by the dancing flames. I watched, hardly daring to breathe; they looted everything, took whatever rations they wanted and pulled everything out of the car. They were there for about two hours: consuming our supply of whisky. They kept the fire going outside the hut and sat in a group with their blankets wrapped around them; it was cold at that altitude at night. I was tempted to creep closer and empty both barrels of the shotgun, but I knew the slightest noise of rustling bushes or stones being disturbed, would have brought down a blanket of withering gunfire against which the bushes would not have provided any defence.

Something about discretion and valour crossed my mind as I lay, as still as possible, with stones as big as my fist digging into my body, and getting colder by the minute in the night mountain air. It was past midnight when the party decided to move on, high on bhung – cannabis or opium – and the remainder of our whisky. With a last random volley of shots into the bushes, they mounted their horses and disappeared into the night. I continued to lay there shivering, half dozing but kept awake by the sound of the nocturnal predators searching for a victim; the noise of the river was continuous. I must have dozed off huddled in a ball against the cold as I woke to the sound of goat bells, with goats all round me nibbling at the shrubbery; they were not perturbed at my presence. The warmth of the sun was indeed welcome and my joints were stiff and my muscles ached from the stones and the cold.

Clutching my shotgun with both barrels cocked I moved in and out among the bushes towards the hut, where I found Trevor surveying the looting and destruction of the previous night. The car was a wreck, all the windows and glass broken, tyres punctured, engine cables ripped out; there had been a feeble attempt, fortunately failed, to set fire to the car. It would have been spectacular if it had succeeded as there were still ten gallons of petrol in jerry cans in the boot. As it happened, the car and fuel were now redundant, it would never move again under its own power. We foraged around trying to salvage what we could; a can of bully, a bag of army hard tack biscuits and a two pound tin of IXL peaches with a scorched label and two blankets from the hut riddled with holes.

There was no sign of my father. We searched the area around the hut, fired shots into the air, hoping for a response, all to no avail. I thought he was dead, shot during the attack the previous night. We questioned the small goat herd, a boy of about ten or twelve years of age, but it was impossible to communicate as he spoke no English and his own language was unknown to either of us. He kept pointing to the mountains in a northerly direction and repeating the word "Bagh". It did not mean anything at the time but I have since discovered it is the name of a village or small town high up in the mountains. The boy moved on northwards, whistling and calling his goats which followed, stopping only to nibble a few leaves here and there with their goat bells tinkling as they went.

Having studied a detailed map of the area since these events, I discovered we were in a triangle of borders: Kashmir, Pakistan and a small independent state called Poonch. I believe we had crossed an undefined border into the latter. The area was mountainous, sparsely populated, unproductive, lawless; a totally feudal society. Banditry was a way of life for these people as with the people of the North West Frontier. They would politely invite you to have a cup of tea and before you had drunk half, have shot you dead. Loyalty and trust extended no further than the immediate family. From the experience of the night before, we realised that we were too vulnerable in the vicinity of the hut with the bridle track so close. We followed the track down to river level for about two miles from the hut, where we joined the main bridle track which followed the course of the river in both directions.

We scrambled directly up the hill, ignoring the river bank track, to a point where we could observe the bridle path coming from the south. Our view to the north was limited by the undulating terrain.

While looking for a suitable place to put down our few possessions, we discovered a shallow cave, or rather an overhang of rock which could afford some shelter. We were about two miles from the hut but three hundred feet higher up the steep hillside. The cave smelt of wood smoke, and the crude fireplace, made with a circle of rocks, was still warm from a recent fire. I surmised the young goatherd may have spent the previous night there. I rested in the cave while my companion returned to the hut to forage around to see if he could retrieve any further rations. He returned with miscellany of items: another tin of bully, with a rifle bullet hole right though the middle, another blanket, also with bullet holes, a pair of pliers from the car tool kit, one pillow which had escaped any damage, and a pair of binoculars rescued from a bush, but with the right lens shattered. They had belonged to my father, for use on his hunting trips, and proved invaluable over the next 20 days. The final item was an empty Johnny Walker whisky bottle.

There was nothing else of any use.

We feasted on hard tack, bully beef and biscuits. Having torn open the damaged tin with the pliers, our hunger was satisfied but we were left thirsty from the dry biscuits.

We punched a hole in the can of peaches and each had a mouthful of the syrup. It was still daylight, the heat of the day had left us parched; we needed water and there was plenty of it, rushing madly, one hundred and fifty yards down the steep slope to the river. After scanning the bridle path both ways for any activity, it fell to me to go down to the river and fill the whisky bottle. Clutching my loaded shotgun, whisky bottle stuffed inside my shirt, I started to descend to river level. If any movement was seen on the path, Trevor would blow his police whistle and I was to take cover until the danger had passed. From our advantageous position, he could see more than a thousand yards of the track downriver, with the aid of the damaged binoculars.

The first excursion to the river was uneventful except that it took me three times as long to get back to the cave than to descend. I had drunk my fill at the river in spite of the remembered vision of dead sheep and, on one occasion, a dead donkey, floating down river at Baramullah, where we regularly went swimming during the summer months, while I was at school there. I think most colonials had developed immunity to tummy bugs which seemed to take a terrible toll against the British troops especially in the first few months of acclimatisation; many soldiers will recall the dreaded Delhi Belly otherwise known as the squitters.

The next two days were quiet in our little hideout. We observed small groups of horsemen approaching from the south, sometimes three, four or five riding in single file along the river bank: most of them took the right hand arm of the fork taking them right past our abandoned hut, in the direction of Bagh.

We didn't dare light a fire for warmth; it would have betrayed our position for miles around. At the end of the third day, we had consumed all our meagre rations including the peaches and were left with a bag full of broken biscuits. We had to eat – a plan was hatched – daring, foolhardy and downright criminal. When self preservation is involved, reason and morals are conveniently suppressed, on a national scale, it would be labelled anarchy.

Chapter 11
The Hide

WE WERE desperate, hungry, dirty, thirsty and very tired from lack of sleep, and above all in danger of being murdered by gangs of ruthless, lawless tribesmen who would have had no compunction in despatching us like a pair of rabid dogs – we had to act first. It was decided we would attack the next group of horsemen coming from the south (there was no activity from the other direction), but we had to take into account the numbers involved. Almost the whole of the fourth day was spent scanning the track for movement, with our one lens spy glass. By mid afternoon two groups had passed our lookout point, but there were too many, about five or six in each troop. In the late afternoon my companion said, "Let's go". He had spotted a group of three mounted men in single file, approaching at walking pace, at a distance of twelve hundred yards.

We had plenty of time to cover the distance to the fork in the bridle track at river level. Dodging, running and jumping behind bushes and huge boulders we reached the fork in a few minutes. The plan was that I should take up a position behind a huge rock half hidden by thick shrubbery and directly facing the oncoming group. I had the shotgun, my heart was pounding and I was a little breathless from the exertion of our hurried decent. Trevor took up his position only five yards behind me, armed with two pistols, mine and his own police revolver. "Don't fire till I blow the whistle," was his last instruction while he also disappeared behind another rock. I was in a crouched position with the barrel resting on the top of the rock well concealed, only daring to peer over the top of the rock for a second or two to observe the trio approaching. One hundred and fifty yards, one hundred yards, seventy five yards, cock both barrels. "Damn they have a dog with them". At fifty yards the dog took over the lead of the party and was twenty yards ahead of the horses. The dog had caught our scent and was advancing to investigate this new odour. "Blast it!" the dog was coming straight for my hide, tail wagging like mad. The dog was nuzzling its way through the bushes, thirty yards, sweat pouring down my back, finger on trigger, blow your bloody whistle, they are nearly on us.

The dog was whimpering, sniffing timidly at my knees, twenty yards, the first horse reared up, also having caught our scent, the whistle blew and I discharged the first barrel, taking out the first two who took the full blast at head height, a slight adjustment of angle and the third man fell while trying to get at his weapon slung across his back. This part of the operation was a bit vague. Trevor despatched the first two riders with his pistol, the third was already dead having taken the twelve bore at chest height. The horses were calm obviously quite accustomed to gunfire. We unsaddled the horses and turned them loose. The dog yelped as the first barrel exploded and disappeared, tail between its legs, but reappeared a few minutes later. The sound of the gunshots reverberated between the walls of the valley; the horses continue to nibble at the verdant grass at the edge of the water. I grabbed the sacks and saddle bags of each horse and recovered what we thought was most useful, tossing the saddlery into the river which soon swallowed up the evidence. The three bodies were also pushed into the river to disappear within a minute in the raging water. Trevor recovered a Mk. IV Lee Enfield rifle and a bandolier of ammunition before unceremoniously heaving the late owner into the river.

It was a struggle up hill, stumbling, slipping, sliding, trying to haul our ill gotten gains back to our retreat. We had to stop frequently to catch our breath, adjust the load, and scan the bridle path in case the shooting had attracted attention. We were at the fork no more than forty minutes, unsaddling the horses, removing the bridles, collecting some of the sacks they had slung over the horses, pushing all that we could not carry into the river. The horses were still there grazing while we were half way up the hill, then as though they knew their way home they took the upper arm of the bridle track and soon disappeared from view heading north by the time we reached the cave. We abandoned some of the sacks as we neared the cave, arms aching, out of breath and adrenalin still pumping from the excitement and tension of the last hour, we just could not have finished that uphill slog. We intended to rest a while and retrieve the sacks before dark. The evening was advanced and the sun was sinking behind the hill on the opposite bank, we had hardly spoken during the climb, only swearing and cursing as we skinned our knees and knuckles as we slipped and slithered on the loose scree, the heavy sacks threatening to drag us down hill again.

Our first action on reaching the cave was to have a long drink of water from the two chuggals – canvas water bottles – and hang them where we could keep them cool. We could not resist the temptation to explore the contents of the sacks; food was our first priority and we were not disappointed. The first sack revealed neatly tied bundles and a container of cooked rice, chapattis (bread) and a well seasoned vegetable stew with pieces of meat which had been well shaken up on the uphill trek. We ate with our fingers, with the minimum of washing, dipping the bread into the stew and scooping up the rice. The food was cold but we were famished after a day and a half without any sustenance, it was more than welcome. We gave little thought as to the method by which we had acquired this banquet. We drank again from the chuggals to cool our mouths and throats from the pungent stew. Having now discovered the valuable cargo in the sacks we could not leave the four sacks where we had left them, some forty yards down the hill. The light was failing and we had to hurry as we would never find them in the dark, and they were far too precious to leave till next morning. We recovered the sacks and returned to the cave feeling more than satisfied with our achievements for that day, in fact we felt quite elated, with no thoughts of remorse.

With two extra blankets we hoped we would be a little warmer during the night, we stored the other sacks in a cool place to be investigated in the morning. Rummaging through the pockets of a jacket of one of the trio, which had been loosely tied to one of the sacks, we found a packet of cigarettes, a lighter, and a small cloth bag with draw strings which revealed two hundred Indian rupees and some loose annas and pice. We lay down early, smoking and discussing our strategy of the day. It was more comfortable now as we had also brought up an army issue type machete with which we had cut more small branches to use as a rough mattress as protection against the hard floor of the cave.

The encounter had been cheap for the quantity of ammunition expended. I had used only two shotgun cartridges. Trevor had fired five pistol rounds. This automatically brought us round to assessing our stocks:

32 shotgun cartridges, 19, 9mm rounds for my pistol and 12 rounds of .45 calibre police issue. In addition we had captured a .303 rifle with a cloth bandolier of about 50 rounds. We did not dare light a fire. Trevor took the first watch while I lay down to a fitful sleep; at least I was not hungry. Although we had not talked about it, I believe that carrying out a stock-take on our ammunition, we had already decided subconsciously that a repeat operation would be necessary if we were to survive. I fell asleep thinking of what fate had befallen my father.

The fifth day since we left Pindi dawned cold with a cloudless sky. We had saved some of the food from the previous day and had agreed to eat only once at midday, breakfast was just a drink of water from the chuggal. Trevor scanned the horizon for any activity, there was nothing to report. We were both eager to explore the contents of the other four or five sacks and a bundle. We found more food, a couple of cheap cotton towels, cigarettes, a full bottle of whisky, an enamel mug, the contents of each sack was roughly the same, more food and an old .45 calibre revolver.

Each sack revealed a smaller drawstring bag which was quite heavy for the size, we emptied the contents onto a towel and were surprised to see an array of silver bangles, anklets, chains and necklaces, above all, solid gold bars. The bars were approximately an inch wide, six inches long and over half an inch thick. We emptied all the sacks: three of them disgorged a similar haul of oriental type jewellery all in solid silver. The heavier pieces were studded with semi-precious stones of various colours and sizes, rubies, lapis lazuli, moonstones and opals, and a total of twelve bars of gold. The bars were quite distinctly embossed "Government of India" a broad arrow stamp and a serial number: other numbers probably indicated weight, purity and date. We were quite stunned by the haul and we wondered how much more we had pushed into the river.

We had enough food for a further three days, water was the pressing need. It fell to my companion to make an emergency trip to the river to fill the two chuggals and whisky bottle, and to dip the towels into the river and bring them back dripping. We would have welcomed Gunga Din as a companion. I would watch the track and I would fire one rifle shot if there was any danger, he was to take cover or return immediately to our hide. It was not necessary, and he was back in forty minutes with the precious load of water and the still dripping towels. Not having washed or bathed for over a week it was a luxury to strip down to underwear and have a rub down in the warm sunshine. We were now looking bearded and heavily tanned from the almost constant exposure to the sun and wind, our clothes were crumpled and dirty and no doubt a bit smelly.

Days five, six and seven were completely inactive for us. Several mounted groups passed below us, all of them taking the upper arm of the track in the direction of Bagh. Day eight found us back at square one with little food left from our haul, and thinking of replenishing our supplies though hardly talking about it. The day ended with stale vegetable stew and leathern chapattis, and confirmed the necessity for another ambush as soon as possible.

By mid afternoon on day nine, the opportunity presented itself. The group consisted of four riders, but being confident from our success during the last episode and the comparative ease with which it had been accomplished, and having an additional weapon, the rifle, we considered the four would not present a great challenge. There were minor changes to our strategy. I would take up the same position; Trevor would move thirty yards further back behind me with the rifle. This time the signal to fire would be when I discharged the first barrel.

We were in our positions with plenty of time to observe the group approaching, quite oblivious of our presence, and no dogs in view to give away our position. As they got closer the excitement induced a faster heartbeat, a cold sweat and trembling. Thirty yards, both barrels cocked, oblique line of fire on the first two riders, grip the stock tighter, the palms of my hands wet and clammy. Twenty yards, one shotgun barrel discharged, a one second delay, a loud report of the rifle shot, two seconds delay – second barrel discharged, the echoes chasing each other down the valley. Four riders and one horse lay on the bridle path. We knew exactly what we had to do, despatch the wounded first, unsaddle the horses, saddle bags and sacks to the side of the track, bodies and saddlery into the river, all arms thrown into the river. The wounded horse had been hit in the neck as it reared up and startled by the gunfire, the rifle bullet passing through and striking the rider in the face. Fortunately the horse had fallen very close to the water's edge and in its struggles, slipped closer to the raging river; the horse was despatched with one pistol shot. Using two rifles like crow bars we levered the carcass closer to the torrent, once the flanks were in the flow, the force of the water assisted in the disposal. The four bodies presented no problem, an arms and legs swing between the pair of us and they disappeared in the raging river.

There was no feeling of remorse or guilt and to this day I am unable to explain the mental blackout at the time. We hurriedly dragged the seven or eight sacks thirty yards up the hill concealing them in the shrubbery. Trevor was scanning the path every few minutes to ensure the coast was clear. We spent almost an hour disposing of the evidence, the dead horse, having absorbed most of the time and energy. What surprised me most was the calmness of the animals; they seemed quite unmoved by the gunfire. I had expected one or two to bolt, but having unsaddled them, they started to graze quite unperturbed.

We now started a relay operation of moving the sacks and water bottles up the hill towards the hide, returning each time to retrieve another couple of sacks till we finally got them back to the hide quite exhausted.

Food was still first priority, we hurriedly rummaged through a couple of sacks pulling out the neatly tied bundles which looked as though they contained food, they did; we shared the contents and drank our fill from the chuggals.

From this point onwards, at the end of day nine, Trevor seemed to fall into a state of sullen depression. The following two days he hardly spoke, just sitting with the spy glass on one side, pistol on the other side, nervously looking down the river for any signs of movement.

We had examined all the sacks – enough food for three days – a couple of blankets and another haul of jewellery, no gold bars in this lot. We put the jewellery and gold bars into the pillowcase from the pillow we had recovered from the car. It was quite heavy and was equal to half a pillowcase and probably weighed twenty pounds or more. It was casually stacked against the rock wall of the hide.

The tenth, eleventh and twelfth days were quite uneventful, only one group of riders passed beneath us taking the same upper arm of the track as all the others had done. It was now late September and the nights were getting distinctly colder, the extra blankets of very coarse goat hair, were a great adjunct to our primitive comfort. The days were still warm, in fact quite hot from noon to just before sunset, there had been no rain during our stay only a fine mist which cleared as the sun got higher in the sky. Trevor was becoming more agitated viewing the track every few minutes with pistol in hand.

The heat of the day and the cold at night quite frequently dislodged small stones from the face of the cliff above us, these usually bounced over us and down the hill quite harmlessly followed by a cloud of dust and a few pebbles falling at the mouth of the hide. At night these sounds were magnified and on two nights in succession I saw Trevor sitting up, pistol in hand, shaking like an aspen leaf, beads of perspiration on his forehead. I was afraid to move in case he fired at me. "Have a cigarette," I suggested fumbling around in the dark for the packet and lighter. I struck the lighter to reveal his face glistening with sweat and his pistol hand shaking so violently he could not have hit anything smaller than a barn. A cigarette and a swig of whisky, very sparingly issued, seemed to calm him down, with the explanation that it could be nocturnal predators hunting for prey – I was justifiably getting jittery myself, afraid that if I moved at night I may be mistaken for an intruder, a .45 bullet at close range leaves no options.

I believed that his extra years gave him the experience to realise that we were in a precarious situation and in greater danger than my boyish years allowed me to consider. I feel now that I had temporarily become detached from reality and considered the whole episode as a game of dare. I was beginning to feel at this time that I should broach the subject of returning to Pindi, but refrained, leaving it to his superior judgement.

On the thirteenth day we made another foray to the fork at river level. There were three in the party and our ambush tactics remained unchanged. Our reactions were now automatic and each one knowing what to do immediately the shooting stopped. We hauled our loot uphill having disposed of the evidence in the usual manner, and having turned the horses loose. In our detached state of mind we seemed to have more compassion for the animals than for the human victims, a very destructive psychological symptom for future years if allowed to continue too long.

We went through the routine which was well established, food first, all other considerations were secondary as we rummaged through the latest haul of sacks. More food, more blankets, more whisky, more jewellery, more bhung, more money and lengths of silk and sari material, presumably for their women.

The evening of the thirteenth day was a turning point in our plans. I plucked up enough courage to broach the subject of our return to Pindi and was surprised that he agreed without any objections. We had to draw up a plan and make preparations for the first leg of the journey back to Murree a distance of about twenty miles, most of it up hill from the main road. It did not take long to pack what we decided was absolutely essential into the sacks which we had in the hide. We put all the jewellery into the pillowcase except for two gold bars, one each, and the pillowcase was tied at the neck end and placed in a sack. A hole was dug using the machete about thirty feet south of the hide and twenty feet below the goat track. The earth and stones were pushed back into the hole covering the sack with a foot or so of rubble. No one could possibly have found it. We agreed that if either of us ever got back to this spot, he would seek out the other, wherever in the world, to share the loot. Our mood was optimistic and spirits were lifted at the thought of getting back to civilisation. We split the money equally about seven hundred rupees each, almost fifty pounds at 1947 exchange rates, enough to keep us going for a few weeks till we knew what the future would bring.

We were now ready to put into operation the second part of the plan, each had his sack packed, an extra sheep skin coat and bundles of food. We were to make one more foray to the fork and use the horses to get back to Murree. Both of us could ride. Trevor had learned as part of his police training and I had learned as a youngster by exercising horses at the Royal Artillery barracks in Rawalpindi where father had been District Magistrate. We were prepared to ride all the way to Pindi if necessary about 70 miles but hoped otherwise.

We sat patiently for the next four days, getting more agitated as the flow of traffic seemed to come to an end and the possibility of having to walk began to loom larger. "We'll wait one day more," said Trevor, "and then we must make a move." A sense of urgency seemed to have crept into his voice, and I was also frustrated at the long wait. We knew we were about three or four miles down river from Kohala and could have taken the lower arm of the bridle track but I wanted to return to the shack for one last look around for signs of my father.

We were up early the following day determined to make a start, as usual Trevor scanned the track for activity, and all he could see was twenty or thirty vultures circling low in the valley. We assumed that either a body, or more probably, the carcass of the horse which would have been bloated by this time, had got wedged close to the bank: we were not about to investigate.

We strapped the sacks to our backs, like haversacks and I stuffed my shoes with material as both shoes had holes in the soles from the rough treatment the previous two weeks. Trevor's police issue boots with hob nails in the soles had fared better and with the chuggals full of water slung at the waist, we were ready to move at short notice.

We were about to set off on foot when Trevor took one last look down the bridle track "They're coming," he said excitedly, still holding the spy glass to his eye. "I can't tell how many there are." He grabbed his sack and rifle and was on his way down hill before I could remonstrate with him. I had no option but to follow, sack, shotgun and jacket brushing and pushing passed the shrubbery. Half way down he stopped to take a look at the track. "Four or five I'm not sure," he said. I was apprehensive; we were getting over confident and letting ourselves in for a gun battle. We took up our usual positions with time to spare, Trevor still frequently viewing the approaching group till he confirmed the numbers, "Five," he said. I was now scared; we had not taken on so many before and if our cover was blown we could end up in a shoot out, out numbered with unpredictable results.

The tactics were to remain the same; I was to fire first, allowing them to approach to a range which had proved so effective in the past. The wait seemed interminable and was accompanied by the usual heart pounding and sweating. I heard Trevor manipulate the bolt action of the rifle, he was not far behind me; I took one last glance back in his direction but could not see anything that would give away his position. I hoped I was equally well concealed.

The last minutes were agonising, the sound of the horses' hooves on the stones and voices were quite clear. It crossed my mind that this group must have passed very close to the carcass of the horse, or a body, which would have been brought to their notice by the vultures and red kites which are reluctant to leave once they have started feeding. At fifty yards I observed that none of the riders had their rifles slung across their backs as the previous groups, but slung from the shoulder or in front of them on the pommel of the saddle. They seemed to be more alert as though they were expecting a rival gang and needed to keep their arms readily accessible.

At twenty five yards I discharged the first barrel, immediately followed by a louder sharper crack from behind me, a second later I emptied the remaining barrel, with a second and third report coming from the rifle. I hastily reloaded. The first three riders had fallen victim to my shotgun. Trevor had taken out the other two, but he continued to fire from his slightly elevated position at a target I could not see. I was not prepared to expose myself to possible retaliatory fire till I was sure the five were out of action.

Trevor fired three more rifle shots and I heard him change magazine (the old Mk. IV could hold six rounds only, one in the breach and five in the magazine). We both remained concealed for a few minutes more. He called out in a soft voice "Are you okay?" "Yes," I replied. "Don't move yet," he added. He then fired two more rifle shots over my head. The horses began to scatter up and down the bridle track but showed no signs of bolting. With the horses out of the way the results of the gunfire were evident; five men lay dead or mortally wounded. Trevor carried out the despatching duty and the bodies were pushed into the river.

We only rounded up three of the five horses; the other two had strayed too far. We unsaddled one horse and turned it loose, disposing of as much evidence as possible. We were not too worried about evidence since we would be leaving the area as soon as we collected our pre-packed sacks. It only remained to decide which arm of the bridle path we should follow. The lower one followed the river and would eventually bring us to the bridge at Kohala, the upper track which would take us to the shack where we were fired on that first night. We chose the lower route as it would be shorter. It was with great relief we mounted the sturdy mountain ponies and set off up river, frequently looking behind to make sure we were not being followed. At walking pace we expected to get to the bridge and customs station in about an hour. The customs stations were about two or three hundred yards further down the tarmac road from where the bridge entered Kashmir territory.

The ride to the bridge was quite uneventful but gave us time to reflect on our wild adventure of the last three weeks, we didn't talk much. Trevor was sullen and I was still in a highly stressed state of mind. I suppose we both had much to think about. Trevor was on the lead horse, I followed a few lengths behind, the horses quite docile and responsive to the reins.

He stopped abruptly and motioned to me to go back and retreated himself and dismounted. I also got off my horse, weapons at the ready, as Trevor was crouching low and leading his pony back along the track signalling me to do the same. We retraced our steps about twenty five yards before he spoke in a low voice. We had almost reached the bridge and the tarmac road, only a hundred yards round the next bend in the path. We tethered the horses to a couple of mature bushes, and crouching, we made our way to a point where we could observe the bridge and survey the customs post.

There was no sentry on either end of the bridge but there was some activity. Tents had been erected and there were soldiers moving around a barrier of tar barrels filled with rocks which had been placed across the main road which indicated to us that no vehicular traffic could pass the border post. The bus service from Srinagar or Rawalpindi had been suspended. The Indian Army had set up a border post with sand bagged positions since our last visit and it would be safe to assume that a similar post had been organised on the other side of the bridge in Pakistani territory. We returned to the horses unobserved to consider what we should do.

There were only three options open to us. Firstly surrender ourselves to the Indian border post and hope they would let us cross the bridge, with the possibility that they would take us into custody and transport us to Srinagar as potential enemies. The second option was to make a dash for the bridge and cross before the border post was fully aware of our presence. With this second choice we had the element of surprise on our side. The last option was to sit tight till darkness fell and sneak our way across with the least risk of being detected. While we debated the possibilities of each option, we decided to eat as it was past midday. We ate, had a cigarette or two, swigged from the chuggals, freshened up with a face splash from the river and watered the horses.

The long wait to darkness ruled out the third option, although the crossing presented the least risk, plus the fact that it would have been suicidal to approach the Pakistani post in darkness. We did not know its location or how far from the bridge it had been established, or in fact, whether one had been set up. The third option was abandoned.

The first option appeared on the surface to be reasonably safe if we could be granted unhindered passage across the bridge. Our appearance, in crumpled clothing, dirty, unshaven and burnt brown would not inspire any confidence in our prospective interrogators. However, if we were arrested and searched as a potential risk, (any excuse to exercise authority), the discovery of the gold bars would have branded us no better than the thugs and bandits from whom we had taken them. The possession of a military rifle would have given rise to even greater suspicion. The prospect of being taken off to Srinagar then Jummu and probably Delhi in chains, as pawns in a political game, a long incarceration in an Indian jail, a show trial with unknown end results, was not a prospect to be dwelt on for too long. Option one suffered the same fate as the third plan.

Having decided to make a dash for the bridge we had to plan our timing. Total darkness was out of the question, late evening when the sun was setting behind the mountains with long dark shadows cast over the valley was preferable. The rush of the river would deaden the sound of the horses' hooves and hopefully an uneventful boring day would have lulled the guards into a feeling of complacency.

We crept back to the point from where we could take a more thorough look at the bridge and customs post, each of us taking turns with the spy glass to pick out any pitfalls in our plan. The sentries seemed quite at ease, smoking, with weapons leaning against the sandbags. A closer look at the bridge revealed barbed wire had been stretched across the entrance to the bridge, we could have entered between the strands but it would have been impossible to take the ponies. "Don't worry," Trevor said, "I brought the pliers somewhere in my sack." Just as we were preparing to retreat to where the horses were hitched we saw the brilliant light of a petromax lamp being hung on a pole outside a marquee tent. It was still quite light but indicated preparations were being made for some activity and the lamp was the focal point.

We returned to the ponies and Trevor spent some time foraging in his two sacks looking for the pliers, which he put in his breast pocket. The shadows were lengthening and the moment of departure was imminent. We were to walk the horses to the bridge keeping them between ourselves and the sentry post, as a shield against possible fire by the sentries. We got to the point where we would be in full view; Trevor put his finger to his lips. The lamp by the marquee seemed brighter and was in our favour as the brilliant glare from the mantle would make it difficult for a few seconds for the eyes to focus on a target two hundred yards away. We had now reached the point of no return, so very slowly, half hidden by the ponies, we started to walk the longest hundred yards of our lives.

With fifty yards to go to the bridge a fire alarm sounded, an old fashioned triangle of metal struck with a hammer. There was immediate activity round the lamp at the entrance to the marquee, fifty or sixty soldiers pushing and shoving, talking loudly and laughing. It was meal time at the border post, a welcome distraction; additional lamps came out increasing the glare to our advantage. We covered the remaining yards to the barbed wire strands across the bridge, the pliers made short work of the first strand which went twanging back, rolling itself rapidly into a tangled ball onto the other side of the road. The second strand took no longer than the first, and we took our first steps on the bridge towards Pakistani territory. Halfway across the bridge two rifle shots were fired, we broke into a run dragging the ponies behind us. I don't know if the shots were actually aimed at us or if they had been fired in the air as a warning that we had been observed. A small group of soldiers appeared at the point where we had cut the wire, brandishing their rifles in the air and shouting (probably abuse) at us, but making no attempt to follow. We were still taking shelter behind the ponies crouched and walking at a quick pace to put as much distance between us and the soldiers at the other end of the bridge and although we were well within range of their rifles, no further shots were fired.

We continued walking, the road almost immediately started to ascend on the way to Murree. The first major bend in the road obscured the view of the bridge and for the first time we felt a little more secure as we were now on familiar territory. It suddenly seemed to get very quiet, the continuous roar of the rushing river, which we had endured for weeks, was screened by the hills around us and the increasing distance from the torrent. Huffing and puffing from the uphill climb and dragging the ponies behind us, and the exertion of the run across the bridge, we just flopped down on the roadside fumbling for the cigarettes and an opportunity to release the tension. We briefly caught the last rays of the sun which lifted our spirits, as it was sinking between two peaks in the west. The dark foreboding shadows would soon envelope us. As we sat there we were startled by a jeep, containing four soldiers, which appeared in front of us, they came silently down hill, probably coasting, the reason we did not hear them. We stood up, arms raised, waving a greeting, we hoped. We were overcome at the welcome of the back slapping, offers of water and a hundred questions.

It transpired we were the first people in weeks to have crossed the bridge from Kashmir. We gave them whatever information we had gained regarding the border post on the Kashmir side and the probable numbers of soldiers. We did not see any evidence of field artillery or anything heavier than light machine guns. Fortunately Trevor had a much better command of Urdu than I had, so he did most of the talking, occasionally glancing in my direction as if to ensure I was agreeing with what he was saying. We failed to mention our sojourn in Poonch saying we had come by various bridle paths from Baramullah. Our explanation was accepted as credible as the mountains on both sides of the valley were crisscrossed by numerous bridle tracks leading to small isolated villages, and the presence of the ponies and our dishevelled state lent further credence to our story. We declined a lift to their border post but said we would walk the couple of miles, requesting that their sentries were warned of our approach as the light was failing and would be dusk by the time we got there. We mounted the ponies and followed the jeep until it was lost in the bends and twists of the mountain road.

Our reception at the post was a warm welcome; we had spotted the lights – hurricane lanterns – at the barriers and knew our journey's end for that day was not far away. Food was made available; two charpoys were produced, so we deduced we were to be accommodated for the night. The questioning continued by the Subedah Major – there was no British Officer at the post – until quite late at night. There was not a lot Trevor could add, notes were being hurriedly made of what he related. I did not say much for fear of contradicting anything he said, which could discredit our account. We had rehearsed our story in great detail on the ride to the camp. We surrendered the rifle and .303 ammunition to the Subedah Major in charge as a sign of good will: the story of how we acquired it was not questioned – our explanation was plausible but bore no relation to the truth. He was more interested in the number of troops, weapons and artillery on the other side of the bridge. The post was an assortment of hastily erected tents, no marquee as a cookhouse, no ablution facilities, 'spades general purpose' was the password for a toilet.

Trevor and I managed a very superficial sponge down from a bucket; we had to dress again in our dirty, smelly clothes as there was no quartermaster's store at this camp. "Tomorrow you will be okay," the Major assured us, as he was intending to send us to the barracks at Pach Murree. He would have sent us that same evening, but it was dark by now and the lights on the jeep were not working.

We slept on a bed for the first time in three weeks and for those who have never slept on a charpoy, I assure you it is more comfortable than any interior sprung mattress.

The following morning we breakfasted on sweet steaming tea and naan bread. The horses and saddlery were gifted to the Major, we collected our sacks and climbed aboard the jeep: last minute instructions were given to the driver and escort. We were to be presented to the adjutant at the barracks along with the hand written report. The jeep laboured up the steep, twisty mountain road – the engine wailing – while the driver, smoking and talking to the escort at ninety to the dozen, nonchalantly with one hand swung the steering wheel from left to right and back again as though the yawning gorges were not there.

Although it was only a short thirty minute drive to the barracks we had spent the entire journey clutching onto whatever hand hold was available as we swayed one way and then the other trying not to look at the edge of the steep ravines just inches away from the wheels. Trevor tried to persuade him to slow down, "Don't worry Sahib Allah is on our side," he replied as he continued his hair raising, high speed dash up the tortuous mountain road.

It was with great relief that we entered the barracks at Pach Murree and were dropped off at the Adjutant's Office. The escort jumped out, report in hand and entered the orderly room. Ten minutes later a Sergeant ushered us in front of the British Administrative Officer who had already summoned his interpreter to translate the report by the Subedhah Major. We presented a pathetic pair in the Adjutant's Office, he pressed a buzzer which was immediately answered by the entry of a British Warrant Officer saluting and, smarter than a new pin, he glared at this ungainly pair. "Take them away and get them cleaned up and bring them back after lunch. Make sure they have no arms". We surrendered our pistols, shotgun and ammunition which I presume were taken to the armoury. We were escorted by the Warrant Officer first to the QM stores. Having expertly measured us with his tape we were issued with two K.D. – khaki drill – jackets, two cotton vests, two pairs of cotton underpants and trousers and other miscellaneous items like socks and 'chapels' – a sandal like slip on shoe. I was grateful for the latter as my own were falling apart, the soles parting company with the uppers.

Carrying all our newly issued kit we were almost frog marched, left, right, left, right – no slouching about the barrack area – to the Sergeants' Mess. Towel, soap, toothbrush and paste being all supplied, we were escorted by the W.O. to the showers. What luxury to have a hot shower, wash our hair and clean our teeth; indeed a distant memory. We lingered in the showers, scrubbing and rescrubbing while the W.O. sat on a stool not letting us out of his sight; it was worth more than his next promotion if he had lost us while we were in his charge.

Towels wrapped around us we were ushered into another room near the showers where we were set upon by two medical corps orderlies to endure the indignity of total decontamination with DDT sprays from head to toe as though we had just emerged from some louse infested institution. Our 'clean up' as ordered by the adjutant was not over yet, we were still not in a fit state to be presented for questioning.

We submitted ourselves to the regimental barbers for a shave and haircut, the latter being short back and sides with the W.O. supervising – a bit more off here and a bit more off there – until he was satisfied we had been trimmed to the regulation standard and then another quick shower, to wash away the DDT powder.

We dressed in our newly issued jackets and trousers – the fit was a credit to the Q.M's tape measure – and except for the absence of any military insignia we could have passed for a couple of squaddies. Every stitch of our old clothing was disposed of, we were permitted to retrieve what we wanted from the sacks, money and gold bars were secreted on our person. I recovered my faithful small pack which contained my discharge papers and little else. Blankets, jackets, towels were all consigned to the local incinerator.

Feeling cleaner and presentable we were allowed to enter the Sergeants' Mess as temporary members, by permission of the PMC – President of the Mess Committee – who was an impressive giant of a man in the guise of the Regimental Sergeant Major (RSM). We eagerly paid for our pints of Murree Brewery beer and bought two or three of our hosts a round for their generous welcome. By this time half the mess knew that I had been a W.O. myself till a few weeks ago and that Trevor was a policeman. The other half were still speculating in lowered tones as to our motives and identity. We dined generously on the sumptuous menu of the day 'Bully Beef in Battle Dress' – BB in batter – with vegetables and dumplings. followed by a gooey mess covered in hot custard, a great change from the cold stew, chapattis and rice of the weeks before.

At two o'clock we returned to the Adjutant's Office with all the ceremonial antics of such occasions. I presented my discharge papers and Trevor his police identity. The Adjutant read aloud the translated report submitted by the Subedah Major: our exit from Kashmir was related in detail and even the ponies got a mention however there was no word of the surrendered rifle. The meeting was short: he did not question us except to satisfy himself regarding our identity. We learnt later in the mess that all British personnel – about forty – had been ordered to return to their parent regiment in Pindi and the command of the regiment was to be handed over to the Pakistani Officers: he clearly did not want a complicated situation on his hands.

He made no promises and we expected none, except that he would deliver us to the Post Office in Murree in the QM's ration truck the following morning. After that we were on our own.

We thanked him for his hospitality, he wished us luck and we left.

Grateful for a good night's sleep and a hearty breakfast we were picked up at the mess with our few belongings. We called in at the armoury and we collected our arms all cleaned and oiled. It was not far to Muree and as instructed the driver dropped us off at the Post Office.

Life in Murree appeared to have returned to near normal, a few enquiries revealed that the communal troubles had ceased, mainly because the minority population – Hindus and Sikhs – had left the town in an endeavour to get to India.

The bus station office was deserted except for a lone clerk surrounded by various parcels and baskets, presumably the next load of cargo outward bound. We had missed the morning bus to Pindi and learned the next bus out would be at two o'clock that afternoon, so we had to hang about for a couple of hours. We bought our tickets and wandered off in search of lunch, the local population paying little or no attention to our presence. The clerk in the bus station had given us directions to a local restaurant where he and the bus drivers ate regularly. All the nice middle class cafes and restaurants, like Lintotts cafe and tea house, were closed and shuttered. The owners had abandoned their businesses and joined the general exodus. Grindlay's Bank and Cox & Kings travel agents were doing a roaring trade to Australia, Canada and England. The colonial territories of the African continent were shunned, except by a few retired long serving British army and Indian Civil Service officers who dreaded having to return to England after thirty, thirty-five or even forty years absence. They would not have been able to adapt to a life without servants, the exclusive clubs and the pampered life that 'colonial lifers' enjoyed.

The African colonies offered a continuation of the life style at that time. Those of the Anglo Indian community who could afford the move wasted no time in deciding to start a new life in any of the red areas – The Empire- that would grant them entry. Regrettably many families had to wait several years before making the transition to a new country. Most were well educated and could offer skills and a commercial and social contribution to the life of the country of their choice. They were in fact among the first wave of immigrants immediately post war.

Trevor and I ate our lunch and sat around for a while with a couple of bottles of Murree beer awaiting the arrival of the bus from Pindi which would then make the return journey that afternoon. We returned to the bus station in good time: there were twenty or thirty passengers waiting to board with an assortment of baskets filled with fruit, mostly apples and cherries, from the fertile vale of Kashmir; how these loads had been smuggled out remained a mystery, other baskets contained chickens and ducks. A rough crate contained wood carvings and ornamental tables inlaid with bleached bone or ivory, carved during the winter months, for export to the ready markets of Pakistan and India.

The bus eventually arrived, hissing steam from the radiator after the long climb from Pindi: the driver bellowed instructions to his assistant who was unloading the bundles and cases from the roof of the bus. There was little respect for the contents of the packages which were thrown off the top onto the passengers who had just alighted and were eager to retrieve their possessions. Those waiting to start their journey were pushing and shoving to make sure their load was taken on board: complete pandemonium is the only way to describe the scene. Having secured two places on the hard slatted seats, we were soon hemmed in by women, children, baskets and bundles. Fortunately my seat was near the opening in the bodywork where the window should have been.

There was an overpowering smell of sweaty bodies, fermenting fruit, cigarette smoke and petrol fumes: we longed for the journey to start so that the movement of the bus would offer fresh air.

Finally, we moved off amid whistle blowing and a blaring horn: the bus feeling and looking most unstable with luggage, cargo and half a dozen passengers secured on the roof of the bus.

The thirty-nine mile winding, twisting road, mostly downhill, to Pindi and the high pitched whine of the engine, soon induced motion sickness: children either fell asleep or were violently sick over the side of the bus. The squealing brakes and blasting horn on every hairpin bend made for a very uncomfortable journey and we were relieved to pull into the forecourt at Pindi station.

Trevor and I had hardly spoken on the journey. There was no mention of the events of the previous weeks: it was as though we wanted to blot out the memory of what had occurred as quickly as possible. We got off the bus as soon as we could, he was going to report to his police station, and how he would explain his absence I don't know. I told him I was going to Lahore by train as soon as possible. We parted company in the yard with a hand shake and with a final wave, he hailed a tonga.

I never did see Trevor again, though I did meet his mother a couple of years later on Oxford Street in London. She had a sad tale to tell of her son's deep depression and hospitalisation.

I wandered into the railway station and at the ticket office sought information of trains going to Lahore. The slow train leaving at 8:00 p.m. that evening would have got me to my destination in the middle of the night: I rejected it, thinking it unsafe to travel after dusk. The next train – the Frontier Mail – left at 9:00 a.m. the following morning. I bought a first class ticket which entitled me to sleep in the waiting room and eat in the dining saloon. I was surprised at the normality of the town after the original disturbances immediately after partition: most of the minority sects had left except for the old and infirm who had been abandoned by their families in the helter skelter rush to get away to India. They were reduced to sleeping on the footpaths and begging for survival.

With time on my hands I took a tonga to visit old family friends. The Savoy Hotel was closed the Rogers having departed since I last saw them. I believe they originated from Kent and returned there after years of colonial service. Ted Smith – Punjab Police – and his family, left for Australia, Ernie King – Attock Oil Company – departed for Australia. I ventured to the Westridge railway colony where the cottages and bungalows of the senior staff were already unoccupied and looking neglected. I began to feel very isolated and alone in the world. Decisions to abandon the life style and possessions (very few had property to dispose of) and to start afresh in a distant part of the empire were hurriedly made sometimes splitting families in different directions. Most had no idea of what to expect or what prospects of employment might exist when they reached their chosen destination. The over-riding factor was fear of what could happen if the local population turned aggressive. Those who were unable to leave due to financial restraints had their fears heightened by being left behind in dimishing numbers.

I returned to the railway station that evening very dejected and saddened by the frantic upheaval which had overtaken the Anglo- Indian community who were the backbone of the Indian Empire and without whom Britain could not have administered such a huge territory and diverse population.

On arrival at the station I found several families already sitting on heaps of luggage, children sleeping on makeshift beds of steel trunks and bedding rolls. There was, in spite of the numbers involved, a hushed atmosphere with emotional exchanges of information of intended destinations and postal addresses for those lucky ones who had relatives already established in their country of choice, a major factor in their own decision. These were the first batch of post Independence refugees, most of the older generation were reluctant to leave but had the foresight to realise that they had to establish a base to which the younger generation could retreat as soon as they were able.

The night was uncomfortable, September is still quite warm at night and the mosquitoes were persistently troublesome. The waiting room was more than full and I had lost the place where I had hoped to spend a restful night in a reclining chair before catching the train the next morning. I slumped down on the floor with my bundle as a pillow and eventually fell into a fitful sleep with small groups of adults talking well into the early hours of the morning.

As the train pulled in, and on time, there was the usual scramble to secure a seat. Not having any heavy luggage I got aboard quickly and hailed a white coated bearer for a breakfast tray of hot porridge, toast, boiled eggs and a pot of tea. There was no pushing and shoving in my first class compartment but the hustle and bustle all along the platform was indicative of the anxiety and at the same time relief at being able to get away on the first part of a journey into the unknown. There was just one family of five in the same compartment heading for Karachi – the only major port for ocean steamers heading either east or west. It was to be a long journey for anyone hoping to embark on a war battered and patched P & O liner. I dozed and the family stretched out on the trunks and slept as they too had been awake all night on the hard floor of the waiting room.

Getting off the train some four hours later at Lahore I was again overcome by a feeling of isolation as it seemed another hundred families were waiting to board the train and join the exodus.

I left the precinct of the station taking a tonga to the police compound just off the Mall where I wanted to meet up with Harry Shaw of the Punjab Police to ask if he had any information about my father. He was not home but his wife and three daughters were. It transpired that Harry and my dad had been in Green's Hotel the day before, splitting a few bottles of beer and that my dad looked well. I made haste to direct the tonga driver to our house, locked up about a month earlier, before we left for Pindi. Harry assured me the situation was returning to normal, trains were running, internal post and telephones were all functioning but there was no longer any cross border traffic with India. This was to remain the situation for many months.

I was anxious to get home, or to what was left of it. Pretty well everything had been looted; the only servant left was the old cook who cried when he related that he could not defend the house against the looters. There wasn't much to take anyway as most of it had been disposed of before my mother left for the U.K. Father had been sleeping on a charpoy with the minimum of bedding and a table fan to ward off the mosquitoes at night. He had returned to work in Lahore Contonment at the CMA'S office, having bought himself a motorcycle.

When he returned home that evening we were both overjoyed to greet each other. We talked for long hours about future plans, the future being no more than three weeks ahead. We discussed the events which had occurred since the night we were separated in the dark up in the mountains. He had joined up with another group seeking safety away from the towns, but his stay was not as long or dramatic. His group opted to follow the river to the town of Jehlum and dispersed to their respective destinations mostly Lahore and Pindi. We never again spoke of those events. He intended to move into Green's Hotel as the house was no longer habitable. Only the old cook remained: the mali (gardener) and dhobi (laundry man) both Hindus, had been murdered by a mob. The landlord of the house had fled to India with his family.

In the event, we both moved into Green's Hotel: the old cook was paid off for his services and loyalty over the years. It was a sad parting as he had been with the family for nearly thirty years, acting as organiser and bodyguard as well when my father went on tour.

I stayed in Green's for a week debating what to do. There was no mail and I gave up hope of getting instructions to proceed to Karachi and from there to Kuwait.

Harry Shaw the Police Inspector called in every evening for a beer with a list of families who had departed that day. His own departure was delayed while he completed the formalities for passport and bureaucratic paperwork in relation to his pension. I had no passport and could not afford to hang about doing nothing for weeks waiting for the appropriate documentation.

A decision was made on the spur of the moment. I would re-enlist in the army and with this intention in mind went to Lahore Contonment Victoria barracks where one of the British regiments was preparing to withdraw from the colony. I was ushered in front of the Adjutant under armed escort, I presented my discharge book, and after much questioning of past military service of dates and places and reasons for wanting to rejoin, I was accommodated in the guard room while further enquiries were made as to my eligibility and identification. It seemed that contact had to be made with GHQ in Delhi by cipher to verify my particulars. It was a long four days, during which time I was fed and watered and escorted by an armed guard every morning to the Adjutant's office for a two minutes interview.

It was the first time I had come in direct contact with a broad Scottish accent as the regiment, if my memory serves me right, was a battalion of the Black Watch. On the fifth day, during my daily interview, I was informed that authority had been received from Delhi and that I should be re-enlisted in the rank of Sergeant in the Royal Army Ordnance Corps. Without much ado I was duly sworn in, hand on bible and with a swift signature at the bottom of the enlistment form, I was committed for a further seven years in the uniformed service of the Crown, with five years reserve liability.

I was soon kitted out, transferred from the guard room to the Sergeant's Mess and private soldiers who only a day or two previously were guarding me with suspicion were now standing to attention with the normal response of "Yes Sergeant" "No Sergeant". I soon fell into the routine of the regiment performing duties of Orderly Sergeant of the day; barrack room inspections and assisting the paymaster with distributing his rupees and annas on the weekly pay parade.

I was not permitted to leave the regimental compound to visit my father who was only a mile away in the CMA'S office, but I did get a message to him to let him know what I had done. I got a reply the following day, delivered by one of the chaps from his office, wishing me a safe journey and that he would follow as soon as possible.

The rumour mill was working overtime and every day a new departure date was circulating. Pack up and stand by to move – stand down, for reasons unknown – the uncertainty had everyone on edge. The regiment, mostly conscripted men, with a compliment of regular soldiers, had already been away from home for a few years and were eager to get away. Added to which the security situation was tense and armed guards patrolled the perimeter day and night, with occasional shots being fired at night to frighten off prowlers outside the wire.

Victoria Barracks was a huge complex of barrack rooms, cookhouses, gymnasiums, stables, workshops and administration buildings. The regiment had retreated into a fraction of the area, fortifying the position with sandbagged posts and barbed wire, in case it was necessary to fight a rearguard action. The railway station was within easy marching distance, regimental transport was loaded and fuelled for the heavy equipment, all else was to be abandoned as soon as a train could be arranged to move the regiment. The shortage of rolling stock of the North Western Railway was due to the fact that most of the engines and carriages were trapped on the wrong side of the border when independence was declared and no organisation existed at that time for the fair and equitable distribution of assets. This was indicative of inadequate planning, and the inexcusable failure to visualise the problems that would arise due to the closing of borders. All resulted from the undue haste with which the withdrawal and shuffling off of responsibility had been initiated, on the one hand, by the Colonial Office and compounded, on the other, by the equally irresponsible attitude of politicians on both sides of the border in their long awaited power grab.

Chapter 12
The Final Weeks

THE STAY AT Victoria Barracks was occupied with mundane routine military tasks of parades, cleaning, packing and unpacking to prevent the troops from getting bored and restless. A major task was to prepare accommodation for the last company of another Scottish regiment who were evacuating Birdwood Barracks in Lahore town prior to handing over the barracks to a Pakistan regiment.

The enclave was now crowded with some twelve hundred men living cheek by jowl, with an increasingly monotonous diet and with N.C.Os urging them on to perform seemingly unnecessary tasks. Sleeping was not comfortable in the crowded barrack rooms with little ventilation, sweltering under a mosquito net, all the punkah-wallahs having been dismissed for security reasons.

I was fortunate in being billeted in the Sergeant's Mess where there were overhead ceiling fans and the meals, with some variation, were edible. Washing and bathing facilities were rationed for the rank and file, the mess offered better facilities.

Finally, word came through that the North Western Railway had managed to muster enough carriages, wagons and a couple of obsolescent engines to move the entire regiment en bloc to Karachi. The train was drawn up at the Cantonment station and the regiment prepared to depart, marching in column, by company, the three miles to the station. I was allocated to the Quartermaster as his assistant for the movement of rations, ammunition and other regimental historical property; all else was abandoned.

Each company of the regiment was preceded by three or four pipers, the company Commanders and Officers marching with their men. The group stretched out for a mile or more on the main road. There were small gatherings of people at the side of the road. Amongst them were those that had a very long association with Victoria Barracks and had depended on the barracks for a living: the char wallahs, chowkidhas, punkah-wallahs, dhobis, boot boys, bhistis with their mussick, each and all a "Gunga Din" in their own right – read Rudyard Kipling – and every soldier was addressed as sahib, no matter how lowly in rank, or how much abuse he had showered on them at some time or another.

Mention must be made of the small group of young ladies, with sad faces and tear stained eyes saying farewell to their boyfriends and their hopes of being a bride. Most of them would have come from the Moghul Pura railway colony where they would have met their soldier boys at the Institute's Saturday night dance.

The troops, well laden down with their kit, arms and ammunition, were singing the barrack room ballads of previous soldier generations who had also served in India.

As the columns of troops marched towards the station, so too did the various groups, keeping pace with them, as though reluctant to let them go, as indeed they were. The troops represented security – a peace keeping, impartial force during communal disturbances and a living link, though incomprehensible, with 'home'.

At the station, each platoon sergeant took a roll call to ensure he had not lost anyone on the way.

Kit and luggage loaded into carriages and goods wagons and it was time to allow the boys and girls their final hugs and kisses and the exchange of mementos and promises to write. The mixed feelings of jubilation at the thought of going home to beloved Scotland was strongly tinged with a feeling of sadness at leaving behind a way of life that can not ever again be replicated.

At last a whistle, a warning to board, and N.C.Os strode up and down the platform urging the lovelorn to part, accompanied by the shouting of various local tradesmen, "Goodbye Sahib", as their source of income moved off. The two ancient engines huffed and puffed to get the heavily loaded train moving. Every window had three or four heads poking out, waving frantically at the slowly receding groups on the platform, until they faded into the distance.

The journey to Karachi was painstakingly slow; the antiquated engines displayed all the evidence of their age and lack of maintenance due to their impending retirement to the breaker's yard. Still on the temporary staff of the Q.M., I was directed to a large goods wagon with four soldiers; this was to be our abode for the next uncomfortable twenty four hours. Half the floor space was occupied with ammunition boxes five high, the other half was our living accommodation. We were all armed and the last order I received was to defend the wagon with my life.

The line to Karachi runs in the southern part of the Punjab, through the province of Sind, one of the driest parts of Pakistan and skirts the edge of the Thar Desert, on the other side of the border. The semi desert was well irrigated by an intricate network of canals, fed from the mighty Indus River, which rose a thousand miles away in the Himalayas.

The steel construction of the wagon made the journey most uncomfortable. The vibrations set up a drumming inside the wagon which was only relieved when the speed of the train was reduced to walking pace. It made communication very difficult plus the heat of the day raised the internal temperature to dehydrating levels. The top half of the stable doors were kept open for the whole journey to allow the air to circulate.

We survived on hard tack rations, bully beef and biscuits and passed through the major towns of Multan, Sukkur and Hydrabad, all situated in the fertile plain of the Indus River, There were innumerable stops – day and night. It was a great relief when the train limped into Karachi where transport was waiting. Fatigue parties were detailed for the unloading, once again roll calls were taken and we were bussed to the huge tented camp situated on the racecourse.

Formalities of checking in and allocation of accommodation were soon completed. I once again, found myself in the Mess enclave surrounded by Senior NCOs from every branch of the service corps – Ordnance, Medical and Engineering – to name but a few. All had been withdrawn from military stations throughout Pakistan; those with families were directed to local hotels.

The busy orderly room published weekly lists of those who were to embark on the troop ships, the points of muster, the dates of sailing and all the relevant information to ensure that the huge task of moving such large numbers of personnel progressed as smoothly as possible. The lists were distributed throughout the camp and there were always groups crowding round the notice boards viewing the list of names: a shout or cheer would go up every time someone found their name, while others with their heads bowed had to endure another period of waiting till the next trooper – troop ship – arrived in port .

Camp life at Karachi was quite tolerable where all the necessities of life were provided, even though they were very basic. There was always a hustle and bustle going on; newcomers coming in and those nominated to embark moving backwards and forwards to the Q.M. stores or the orderly room, either drawing up or handing in bedding or presenting clearance chits. Above all, the checking of medical clearance certificates was imperative: one case of small pox or cholera could quarantine a ship and the whole complement for weeks. Every department was busy with its own aspect associated with the embarkation of a thousand bodies.

Warning signs were posted in all dining marquees, canteens, toilets and ablutions, regarding the smuggling of war trophies and the penalties if caught. The military police were prepared to overlook any offence of illegal arms, grenades, bayonets and pistols if they were surrendered before proceeding on board. I was glad that I had given my pistol to my father for his self protection.

The days ran into weeks and with the population of the camp dwindling rapidly, I began to wonder anxiously when my turn would come. The ships came and went and another thousand individuals disappeared from the camp amid cheering and singing as the convoys left for the port of Karachi.

The withdrawal of the British Army from the sub continent was achieved without chaos or even occasional disorganisation, in spite of the complexity of the logistics problems and the high degree of co-ordination required between the various departments. Great credit was due to the Head Quarters staff at Delhi and Rawalpindi, whose efforts reflected the accumulated expertise of administration from the time of the East India Company, where the movement of troops entailed convoys of bullock carts, camel trains and endless marching.

At long last, my name appeared on the approved list. I don't know if I was relieved, saddened, joyous or just bewildered. The last time I had been in England had been twelve years previously in 1935-36. I was just a boy of ten years of age and can remember the disastrous fire at the Crystal Palace, the abdication of Edward the Eighth and watching the boat race, when in my excitement I fell into the river and was hauled out by a policeman, very wet and cold.

With still a few days to embarkation day, there was no great urgency to obtain all the required clearance chits before finally obtaining the yellow pass, strung around your neck, which allowed you to ascend the gang plank.

The great day dawned, starting with an early parade for a final roll call. With my kit bag slung on my shoulder, webbing equipment packed to bursting, I experienced a feeling of elation matched by the belief that all the waiting around had been worth while. At the same time, there was a wave of sadness. The short journey to the port was over even before I had managed to get comfortable on the hard benches in the truck. We alighted at the shed where there were hundreds of soldiers laying out their kit for a final search by military police for illegal arms. Having cleared that hurdle, we were directed to the quayside where the white painted hull of M.V Empire Ken loomed above us. It seemed huge from our lowly position on the quay but in fact it was no ocean liner, but a wartime captured German cargo steamer converted to a troop carrier. By four o'clock the same afternoon, more than a thousand souls, including families had been embarked.

Allocated a bunk on the deck set aside for Senior NCOs, with my kit stored in a locker and a quick exploration to locate the toilets and ablutions, it was time to return to the fresh air of the upper deck. The troops were directed to the lower decks which were probably cargo holds before the conversion. The ventilation was feeble, the air being thick and heavy with the smell of diesel fumes and pungent disinfectant which induced a nauseous feeling even before there was any motion. The open decks were crowded with bodies, four deep, looking over the railings at the quay side, which was devoid of movement except for a few military policemen at strategic points and a few coolies loading last minute supplies of fresh vegetables. A white painted flag pole, the union flag fluttering weakly in the evening breeze as if it too, was sad at the impending departure and remained the last reminder of years of glory.

Then, from the huge sliding doors of the shed, the regimental pipes and drums band emerged – to the cheers and whistles of the troops almost falling over the rails of the rust streaked sides of the ships in their enthusiasm. The band dressed in tropical tops, but with regimental kilts and accoutrements, marched and counter-marched the length of the quay, the brilliant white blancoed belts and spats emphasising the precision of their marching. The drum major strutted in the lead and directed the band with well rehearsed movements of his mace.

The singing almost drowned out the tunes of the pipes, till a long blast on the ship's horns heralded imminent departure; a slight vibration throughout the ship, a churning and turbulence of the water, another blast on the horns and the distance between ship and quay increased almost imperceptibly. A single corporal marched smartly to the flag pole, saluted the flag and began to lower it very slowly while the band beat 'Retreat.'

The ship fell silent in the reverence – understanding the enormity of the occasion

The vibrations in the ship's structure increased, the distance between ship and quay continued to widen, the water churned to a muddy brown, with a swirling of dock rubbish on the surface.

One more blast on the horn, the bow pointing out to sea, the band still playing on the quay side, the sound fading, the corporal respectfully folding the flag, the ship's complement reduced to a hushed murmur and the crimson sun poised above the horizon of the Arabian Sea – a tangible vision.

Then, as a last gesture of jubilation, a single soldier removed his headgear and flung his solar topee like a Frisbee; it seemed to float on a thermal, followed by a huge cheer and whistling and a thousand topees descended into the water from every deck level.

There was nothing else anyone could do, except, to the fading sounds of the national anthem, say, "Farewell Raj."

Glossary

B.M.H.	British Military Hospital
BABOOL TREE	Camel Thorn Tree
BERIES (Bedis)	Crude rolled tobacco leaf
BHISTIS	Water Carrier
BHUNG	Cannabis
BURKHA	All enveloping robe worn by Muslim women
CHAPLEES or CHAPAL	A sandal slip on shoe with heel strap
CHAR/CHARAY	Tea
CHARPOY	A string bed
CHICO	Small boy – son
CHOWKIDHARS	Night Watchmen
CHUGGALS	Canvas water bottle
COOLIES	Porters
DAK BUNGALOW	Literally post bungalow – rest house
DHAL-AND-CHARWAL	Lentils and rice
HAVALDHAR	Indian rank of Sergeant
JHEEL	A lake formed by the overflow of river during the monsoon season
K.D.	Khaki drill material for uniforms
KHANSAMA	Cook come house boy
MALI	Gardener
MARO SALA	General urging to kill
MEMSAHIB	Lady – Madam
MUSSICK	Goat or calf skin for carrying water
N.C.O.	Non Commissioned Officer
N.W.R.	North Western Railway
NAIK	Indian rank of Corporal

PUNJAB	Divided province between India and Pakistan
PUNKAH-WALLAH	Fan operator
Q.M.	Quartermaster
SAHIB	Gentleman – Sir
SUBEDHAR MAJOR	Indian rank of Captain
SEPOY	Indian rank of Private Soldier
SOLAR TOPEE	Pith Helmet – Sun Hat
STOOD DOWN	Relaxed from the alert position
SUBEDHAR	Indian rank of Lieutenant
TONGA	Horse drawn passenger vehicle
TOPEE	Hat
TUM TUM	Horse or mule drawn cart
URDU	Local Punjab Language
V.C.O.	Viceroy's Commissioned Office
W.O.	Warrant Officer